DIALOGUES AMONG CIVILIZATIONS AND CULTURES

QUESTIONING JEWISH CARIBBEAN IDENTITY

DIALOGUES AMONG CIVILIZATIONS AND CULTURES

Additional books and e-books in this series can be found
on Nova's website under the Series tab.

DIALOGUES AMONG CIVILIZATIONS AND CULTURES

QUESTIONING JEWISH CARIBBEAN IDENTITY

KAREN CARPENTER

nova
science publishers
New York

Copyright © 2018 by Nova Science Publishers, Inc.

All rights reserved. No part of this book may be reproduced, stored in a retrieval system or transmitted in any form or by any means: electronic, electrostatic, magnetic, tape, mechanical photocopying, recording or otherwise without the written permission of the Publisher.

We have partnered with Copyright Clearance Center to make it easy for you to obtain permissions to reuse content from this publication. Simply navigate to this publication's page on Nova's website and locate the "Get Permission" button below the title description. This button is linked directly to the title's permission page on copyright.com. Alternatively, you can visit copyright.com and search by title, ISBN, or ISSN.

For further questions about using the service on copyright.com, please contact:
Copyright Clearance Center
Phone: +1-(978) 750-8400　　　　Fax: +1-(978) 750-4470　　　　E-mail: info@copyright.com.

NOTICE TO THE READER

The Publisher has taken reasonable care in the preparation of this book, but makes no expressed or implied warranty of any kind and assumes no responsibility for any errors or omissions. No liability is assumed for incidental or consequential damages in connection with or arising out of information contained in this book. The Publisher shall not be liable for any special, consequential, or exemplary damages resulting, in whole or in part, from the readers' use of, or reliance upon, this material. Any parts of this book based on government reports are so indicated and copyright is claimed for those parts to the extent applicable to compilations of such works.

Independent verification should be sought for any data, advice or recommendations contained in this book. In addition, no responsibility is assumed by the publisher for any injury and/or damage to persons or property arising from any methods, products, instructions, ideas or otherwise contained in this publication.

This publication is designed to provide accurate and authoritative information with regard to the subject matter covered herein. It is sold with the clear understanding that the Publisher is not engaged in rendering legal or any other professional services. If legal or any other expert assistance is required, the services of a competent person should be sought. FROM A DECLARATION OF PARTICIPANTS JOINTLY ADOPTED BY A COMMITTEE OF THE AMERICAN BAR ASSOCIATION AND A COMMITTEE OF PUBLISHERS.

Additional color graphics may be available in the e-book version of this book.

Library of Congress Cataloging-in-Publication Data

ISBN: 978-1-53614-437-6

Published by Nova Science Publishers, Inc. † New York

In memory of my parents:
Arthur Ernest da Costa Carpenter & Norma Elaine Harty Carpenter

CONTENTS

Preface		ix
Acknowledgements		xiii
Chapter 1	Who Is a Jew	1
Chapter 2	Jewish Identity	27
Chapter 3	The Caribbean Experience	47
Chapter 4	Modern Adaptations	73
Chapter 5	Jewish Lives, Jewish Loves	87
Chapter 6	Conclusion	99
References		107
About the Author		115
Index		117

PREFACE

The subject of this book is the Jewish Caribbean experience from slavery to the present and how Jewish identity is variously understood by those who claim this identity in the islands. *Questioning Jewish Caribbean Identity* lends a fresh interpretation to why various individuals and groups identify with Judaism as lineage, as a religion and a culture. It documents the tremendous impact that Jews have had on the growth and development of industry and modern commerce in the islands, despite their relatively small numbers. It also explores why a religious practice, which in the Caribbean lacks the frenzy, pomp and ceremony of other religions, should have any appeal to so many who have been grafted onto the original Jewish vine over the past 500 years. Transported on the seas from Spain and Portugal in the 1500s while fleeing persecution and the Inquisition, and later during the second wave of exodus from Germany, France and other parts of Europe under threat of World War II, the Caribbean provided safe harbours for a number of Sephardic and Ashkenazi Jews. Their contribution to their new island homelands has been a lasting one. From the technology for the cultivation of sugar, and the development of trade and commerce across the Atlantic, to the Arts and Education. Jewish life within the region has left and continues to leave an indelible mark. The present work begins each chapter with a brief anecdote, intended to illustrate the path that led to the writing of this book. There have been many stops along the way, as I have travelled and interacted with Jews across the globe. These encounters were the genesis of the questions I have asked myself about Jews of all descriptions. Indeed, many of the questions and their answers arise from an existential need to rationalise my own thoughts about my personal identities. This is a pattern I have noted among a number of the theorists included in this work. From Erickson with his Danish-Jewish background and subsequent elaboration of his Psychosocial Theory; to Stuart Hall's Cultural Theory, born out of his own mixed heritage and later inter-ethnic marriage; and Nathan Blumenthal, who changes his rather Jewish name to Nathaniel Branden as he becomes known for his *Psychology of Self Esteem*. We cannot of course speak of identity without acknowledging the seminal contribution of Freud's Psychoanalytic Theory as a way of making meaning of ourselves in the world. Common to all of these theorist, and many others we will encounter in the course of this book is their own struggle with national, personal and ethnic identities. Claiming an identity suggests an autonomous act of loyalty to the chosen identity, and for some can mean the abandonment of previous ways of seeing themselves. This is the central threat of acts of identity, it signals, 'I am with them' and equally, 'I have no allegiance to you. It is the stuff over which battles are waged, and people who appear indistinguishable from each other, obliterate neighbouring nations. This book is a story of the survival of a people, practice, culture, religion

Chapter 1 begins by providing a brief look at the "who is a Jew" law in Israel. It then moves to a historical look at the exodus from Europe and arrival of the first, and subsequent Jews in the various islands of the region. The Caribbean is unique in bringing together the descendants of European explorers and adventurers from Spain, England, France, and the Netherlands; the enslaved people of Africa, the indentured people of Ireland, India and China, and the exiled people of Spain, Portugal, Eastern Europe and Germany. We explore the Jewish presence in the four distinct islands language groups of the Dutch, English, French and Spanish Caribbean. We also take a brief look at the contribution of the Jews in bringing about some of the lasting economic changes to the New World.

Chapter 2 considers the question of identity from a psycho-social and cultural perspective. It looks at what identity is, versus identification and how *Others* affect our view of ourselves. The polemic of the hyphenated identity is discussed in the context of Jewish identity. We also examine self-concept as it relates to the sexual self, within a culture where creolisation is valued.

In *Chapter 3* we consider what being a Jew means for members of the Caribbean community by sharing in the identity of four observant Caribbean Jews. Each of them comes to their sense of Jewishness in different ways. Abrahm Ben Emanuel, Seth, Miriam and Rueben give us a glimpse of what it means for them and the journey they have each taken. These are deeply personal experiences that echo the sentiment of other Jews across the globe. The question of culture as a transmitter of Jewish ideals is considered as a new perspective.

Modern Adaptations - *Chapter 4*, outlines two of the more well know movements that have sprung up in the Caribbean region and which are taking root across the globe. The Rastafari – who call themselves the Black Jews and the Chabad – who have set up offices and institutions in 14 islands of the region. These two groups are at opposite ends of the Jewish continuum and for the region, represent two extremes. As their footprints grow it seems important to examine their mission and possible appeal.

Chapter 5 takes a more romantic turn to look at some of the instances in the historical records of intermarriage, concubinage and the early social practices of the Jewish men of the 1700s and their non-Jewish partners. It also takes a brief look at two modern Caribbean Jews who share their joy and sorrow in both love found, and love lost.

Finally, *Chapter 6* returns to the question of psychology, identity, and religion. It examines how psychology has moved from the notion of the study of the soul to that of a study of behaviour as its new definition. This chapter also considers the move away from religion worldwide towards a more spiritual sense of *Tikun olam - heal the world*, in our daily lives. We suggest that there is hope for a Jewish identity that embraces spirituality and philosophy, and culture as a way forward for younger generations globally.

ACKNOWLEDGEMENTS

I am indeed grateful to those persons who gave of their valuable time and histories in helping me to complete this small glimpse into the life of Jews in the Caribbean. To all who have shared something of their life and mission, my sincere thanks.

Chapter 1

WHO IS A JEW

INTRODUCTION

I went to study in Israel in the late 1980's. My time there coincided with the arrival of the Beta Israel from Ethiopia. When I visited with them I saw yet another cultural expression of Judaism. This image stayed with me until I returned to Israel some ten years later. By then, I could see how much the second generation of young Beta Israel had become a part of the daily fabric of Israel. I walked through the old city in Jerusalem, heading through Jaffa gate. I exited the gate into the city as two Rabbi's passed each other going in opposite directions, the Rabbis nodded in acknowledgement of each other, and I captured the moment in a photograph. One Rabbi was Beta Israel and the other was European. Today, the major cities in Israel are so cosmopolitan that I am indistinguishable from local Jews and people address me in Hebrew. The face of Judaism has been changing for as long as there have been Jews. The history of exodus and exile is part of the Jewish reality and wherever there has been an exodus there has also been intermarriage and assimilation going as far back as Abraham and his wives Sarah and Ketuba and his concubine Hagar. Judaism has survived the atrocities of forced migration, due in part, to the willingness of its tribes to graft others onto itself.

Questioning Jewish Caribbean Identity is a psychological look at the ways in which individuals in the Caribbean experience themselves as Jews. Its starting point is, "What does being a Jew mean to this individual?" (Meyer, 1972, 9). And while Meyer's lens may be historical, mine is the lens of the psychologist, interested in the individual's construction of the self, and how they experience this Jewish component of their identity in community. We come to a sense of who we are not only through community and the social context, but also through our own inner struggles as we try to assert each component of our self-concept. We start off developmentally as part of a mother - father - child unit, which may include other siblings and as we grow and develop mentally and emotionally we find the need to strike out on our own, to both belong and distinguish ourselves from the rest of the family. The psycho-social process of defining and cementing an individual identity begins in childhood and continues throughout our lifespan. In childhood we begin to assert ourselves by establishing *autonomy vs shame & doubt* (Erikson, 1980). The healthy toddler makes every effort to claim their autonomy by attempting to do as much of possible for themselves, learning from their mistakes as they go along. Later when we move into adolescence we are confronted with a prime opportunity for self-discovery and self-identity. In fact, we could say that the onset of puberty marks the biological imperative to become who we will be in the world for some time to come, and who we will be in relation to our significant others. It is the period of great upheaval for many, as well as great opportunity for self-determination. It is no coincidence that the rites of passage such as the *bar and bat mitzvah* take place during this turbulent period. Developmental Psychologist Erik H. Erikson, a Dane and a Jew, describes this critical period as, *identity vs role confusion* when adolescents are, "…sometimes curiously, even morbidly concerned with what they appear to be in the eyes of others as compared to what they feel they are" (Erikson, 1980, p. 94). The ego identity that we develop during adolescence has a great impact on our healthy self-esteem. The positions we hold, the positions we defend in our teen crusader years remain with us throughout adulthood, albeit with less intensity. Each new stage of psychosocial development puts the central question of identity back in play, who am I as a son, father, brother, neighbour, member of the greater community and how do I experience and express this sense of myself in each context. It is the question we answer for ourselves and others when we declare any aspect of our identity, when we declare ourselves Jewish. The additional question that follows is "How are you Jewish?". This is what this book sets out to answer from the phenomenological and personal experiences of individuals, defined by and bound to their Caribbean contexts (Husserl, 1925). This is an exploration of how Jewish communities in diaspora have held on to their sense of Jewishness in the Caribbean region, where their settlements flourished and even where they have left behind traces but no living memory.

Psychologist, Raymond Buriel puts it succinctly when he says,

> The psychology of ethnicity is perhaps the most important because, regardless of variations in the biological, cultural and social domains, if a person self-identifies as a member of a particular ethnic group, then he or she is willing to be perceived and treated as a member of that group. (Buriel, 1987, p. 137).

We are taking ethnicity to mean a combination of culture and those phenotype characteristics which are perceived by others as denoting a racial group. "Culture includes such things as religion (beliefs and rituals), language, music, dress, food, customs, names and naming" (Alleyne, 2002, p. 9). Signifiers such as skin colour, beliefs, behaviours and artefacts have come to be associated with the concept of race. These racial concepts and the cultures in which they thrive along with features of culture such as, "world view, kinship systems, values and morality" all combine to create ethnicity (Alleyne, 2002, p. 9). The fear of assimilation is particularly poignant when we consider the centuries of discrimination, persecution and exile that Jews have suffered globally throughout history. There however, is no long line of people rushing to self-identify as Jewish and no wholesale recruitment in modern times of would-be Jews, so it remains of interest why so many, so far away from any glimpse of a Jewish nation, a Jewish land, still actively preserve a Jewish presence in the Caribbean Sea. Gordon Lewis – historian, notes that in the West Indies the suffering of the Jews was recognised by the Black population as a shared experience that set them apart. Even more poignant is the sentiment documented by Lewis among Caribbean Blacks as early as 1899, that both themselves and the Jew had come through a history of exile and suffering at the hands of the White man. They had both survived, they had come through, "… the valley of the shadow of death, through a land that no White man has passed through, and where no White man has dwelt., and the misery and loneliness of it all is still with them" (in Lewis, 1968, p. 66). Lewis goes on to point out the psychological parallels between the Caribbean Black and the Jew. Indeed, in the United States where some 60 years later the Civil rights movement was to be born, the support of Jews was noticeable in the fight for desegregation and equal rights (Diner, 1995). Jewish and Black literature have reflected the themes of exile, exodus, and the quest for belonging to a homeland. French-Caribbean, psychiatrist Frantz Fanon, interrogates these themes in his *Black Skins White Masks*, and the ways in which the Black man struggles with identity both at home in Martinique (a department of France) and as son of France in the "motherland". Fanon confronts the existential questions of identity from its core level as a personal, psychological experience of self and as a social construct in the ways we experience others. The challenges of identity as a nation and an individual are explored in that work. He argues for a new humanism in which he joins with his brother the Jew in suffering. His stance reflects the influence of his own philosophy teacher who advised…

> Whenever you hear anyone abuse the Jews, pay attention, because he is talking about you. And I found that he was universally right-by which I meant that I am answerable in my body and my heart for what was done to my brother. Later I realized that he meant, quite simply, an anti-Semite is inevitably anti-Negro. (Fanon, 2008, p. 92)

The point Fanon makes here is that an injustice to one, on the basis of difference, is an injustice to all. And difference is not only signalled through skin colour, dress and custom, but it is also what someone else perceives to be different about you that marks you for discrimination. This is what Erik

Erikson would term, "pseudospeciation" (Erikson, 1980, p. 59). It is the psychological process by which groups develop an identity around religious beliefs, culture, national identity, and which allows the group to say who they are, how they are different from others. They then consolidate this *in-group* identity further by viewing others as alien, as foreigners. The reasoning follows that if these others are foreigners they are also inferior. It provides a rational immunity to the acts and beliefs of the foreign group, while insulating the *in-group* from seeing itself as in any way degenerate. It is a brand of xenophobia, directed at the *others*, for their exclusion. Once this worldview becomes a shared mind-set, all the *in-group* acts of discrimination are now justified by their superior psychological stance. It does not take much to see how this pseudospeciation has been applied to ethnic groups throughout history and in particular to Jews and people of colour. Given the history of these two groups, of which Fanon spoke earlier, it is puzzling to understand why anyone who had options to identify with a less victimized group, would want to be seen as both Jewish and a person of colour. Notwithstanding this, it is the case of many of the present descendants of the original Sephardic, Ashkenazi, Marrano and Crypto Jews who came to the Caribbean during their expulsion from Europe and the period of the Inquisition in Spain, Portugal (1492-97) and later from Brazil (1536-1654).

THE CARIBBEAN JEW

> For the Jew in the modern world Jewishness forms only a portion of his total identity. By calling himself a Jew he expresses only one of multiple loyalties... Conscious of an influence which Jewishness has upon his character and mode of life, he tries to define its sphere and harmonize it with the other components of self. (Meyer, 1972, p. 8)

The answer to the question, "Who is a Caribbean Jew?" is not a single answer, nor does it have the same answer each time. The answers to this central question depends on a number of factors. First, I would say it depends on who you are asking, why you are asking and what both parties actually understand by the word Jew. If their intent is religious they may be asking the question, "What does Caribbean Jewish religious practice look like?" or they may be asking from the perspective of ethnicity, "How can I tell if a Caribbean person is a Jew by looking at her?" and still further the individual might want to know, "What political and social views do Jews in the Caribbean support?" or "How does a Caribbean person become a Jew?" Inherent in all these questions is the misconception that there is such a thing as a homogenous group called "The Jews" and that their history is a brief and uncomplicated one. The answer to these questions could include the Orthodox Jew, born of a Jewish mother, is a religious Jew and does not generally see Judaism as a culture or a process of conversion. Or we could just as easily divide the religious Jew into other categories: orthodox, conservative, progressive, reform and reconstructionist Jews. Still others who are seen as Jewish or claim a Jewish identity accept a broader concept of, *bnei Israel*, which recognizes the Jewish family worldwide or the Jewish people - *am Israel*.

More than fourteen million people today claim to be Jews (http://www.jewishvirtuallibrary.org/jewish-population-of-the-world) and the Americas is said to be home to approximately 6,469,500, of that number the Caribbean makes up a fragment. Taking into account Buriel's definition of what constitutes the psychology of identification as an ethnicity, perhaps the most straightforward, nonorthodox answer to, *who is a Jew* is a simplification that recognizes Jew by heritage/birth, Jew by religion/conversion, Jew by cultural observance. The Halachic tradition recognizes the Jew born of a Jewish mother, and those who convert through orthodox Rabbinical practices. The Jew by religion practices his/her Judaism through the belief, rites, celebrations of the Jewish liturgy. While the Jew by culture observes Jewish practice and may be a Jew by birth but secular, a Jew by religion could be a convert or a Jewish and gentile couple where kosher and religious practices are observed.

The differences between the Jews themselves have been made much of. It has been said that there is no homogeneity among Jews, that one section is bitterly opposed to the other. The Western Jews are different from the Eastern Jews, the Sephardim from the Ashkenazim, the Orthodox from the Liberals, the everyday Jew from the Sabbath Jew (to use a phrase of Marx). This also there is no need to deny. But it does not by any means preclude the possibility of common Jewish characteristics. Is it so difficult to conceive of wheels within wheels? Cannot a large group contain lesser groups side by side? (Werner. Kindle Locations 3775-3787, 2015).

THE JEWISH STATE AND THE LAW OF RETURN

Enter Rabbi Itamal Tubul, Head of the Chief Rabbibate's Personal Status and Conversions Division - Israel whose job it is to determine if those seeking return - *Aliyah*, to the state of Israel actually qualify to hold the official status of "Jew".

In 1950, Israel's Knesset passed a remarkable law, beginning with a few simple words that defined Israel's central purpose: "Every Jew has the right to immigrate to this country..." (The Jewish Agency for Israel, (http://www.jewishagency.org/first-steps/program/5131)

At the heart of this debate is the issue of whether or not assimilation is something Jews need to get used to and embrace or whether it heralds the extinction of the Jewish ethnicity as we now know it. "Who is a Jew? This question is becoming ever more pressing for Jews around the world. It looks like a religious issue, but it is bound up with history, Israeli politics and the rhythms of the diaspora" (The Economist, 2014). And so, begins our exploration of this question in the Caribbean.

The "Who is a Jew Law" has been a contentious and divisive issue in the face of a state that is constantly in the process of rebuilding and welcoming immigrants. The question itself has however been relevant for as long as Jews have existed, have been singled out, and have chosen to set themselves apart from others. In the context of this book, the issue is not to make decisions about who qualifies as a Jew, nor to perpetuate a stereotype that has been popularized about what a Jew looks like, how a Jew lives and worships, but rather to challenge that stereotype by exploring the experiences of Jews outside of that context. For many, the words Jew and Israeli are synonymous. Yet for Jews all over the world Israel may be a dream, but not their day to day reality. Most Jews I have interviewed have a tremendous respect and affinity for *Eretz Israel* - the Jewish state, while simultaneously accepting that wherever they find themselves, they are one hundred percent Jewish, regardless of their nationality. The nationality in many cases has been through a happy accident of their ancestors finding safe haven in a welcoming country, far from the dictates of Israel. And yet individuals are inseparable from the culture in which they find themselves. In fact, culture is portable because wherever groups of people preserve their distinctive language, food, dance, beliefs and customs, they also separate themselves from others through their differences.

Undoubtedly one of the key ingredients of Jewish longevity has been its stubborn resistance to letting go of the remnants of culture that survived the various migrations. Ellen Gruber remarks on the seeming reification in Europe of all things Jewish. An apparent obsession to preserve and celebrate any reminders of Jewish history in that part of the world. This is most probably a global trend, and the response of groups of transplanted Jews and their descendants in the face of an awareness of how close the danger of extinction always is.

> As part of this trend, Jewish culture – or what passes for Jewish culture, or what is perceived or defined as Jewish culture – has become a visible and sometimes highly visible component of the popular public domain in countries where Jews themselves now are practically invisible. (Gruber, 2002, p. 5)

THE DIASPORIC EXPERIENCE - SCATTERED ON THE SEAS

The arrival of the Jews in the Caribbean has been documented in various texts (Arbell, Kritzler, Delvante) and is now reasonably well-known among Jewish historians. Yet, for the non-Jewish Caribbean people, who have only maintained a stereotype of the white, frugal, wealthy Jew, they are unlikely to know the history of the Jews arrival in the Caribbean. The journals of Christopher Columbus - Don Colon's, voyages to the New World provide, evidence of the expulsion of the Jews from Christian Spain, from the very first entries. Spain was in a period of expansion at the time of Don Colon's voyages. Along with the expansion of its territories came the compulsory observance of Christianity. Three main events between 1492 and 1496 were to mark the new era of Jewish conversion and subsequent dispersion in Spanish territories. The first was the Alhambra Decree in March of 1492, which demanded the expulsion of the Jews from Castille, giving them four months to leave or convert. On July, 30th of the same year 200,000 Jews were forced out of Spain. Queen Isabel of Spain took possession of Granada and the Moors were forced to accept Christianity. King Manuel of Portugal married Isabel in 1496, occasioning another purging of Jewish influence on the newly converted Jews. All but eight Jews remained and converted to Christianity, at least, on the surface of things (Hakluyt Society, 1813). Columbus' journey to a new world was an auspicious sign and an opportunity for many of the Conversos to leave for a new beginning far from the persecutions of Europe.

THE NEW WORLD – ASSIMILATION AND SURVIVAL

Friday, 3rd August.
    We departed on Friday, the 3rd of August, in the year 1492, from the bar of Saltes,1 at 8 o'clock, and proceeded with a strong breeze until sunset, towards the south, for 60 miles, equal to 15 leagues2; afterwards S.W. and W.S.W., which was the course for the Canaries. (The Hakluyt Society, Journal of Christopher Columbus, 1813, p. 18)

(Google images)

Columbus himself exalts Queen Isabel in the opening paragraphs of his Journal while declaring the great purpose of his expeditions as furthering the Christian cause of the Spanish crown. He addresses Queen Isabel and King Ferdinand as "Catholic Christians and Princes who love the Christian faith..." and who have, "...turned out all the Jews from all your kingdoms and lordships in the same month of January..." (The Hakluyt Society, 1813). Columbus set forth on his most holy mission with those Jews who had very recently and hurriedly converted including his interpreter, Luis de Torres, who was born a Jew. Two Conversos – De Santangel and Sanchez, had helped Columbus finance the voyage. He received technical assistance from two other Jews, namely Zacuto and Vecinho. Despite his exaltations to the crown Columbus was a practical man. This was the beginning of the settlement of the Sephardic Jews from Spain (Sepharda). The colonies themselves were to undergo a series of changes, passing from one colonial crown to the next. The chief protagonists who took possession of Latin America and the Caribbean were the Spanish, the British, French, and Dutch. The lands they laid claim to and which became home for the Jewish Diaspora include those of particular interest for us here. These are Haiti, Santo Domingo, Cuba, Jamaica, Suriname, Curacao.

The settlements in the Caribbean included the French island of Haiti, the Dutch islands of Surinam, Curacao, the British islands of Barbados and Jamaica, The Spanish island of Santo Domingo. All of these islands still have communities of practicing Jews with the exception of Haiti. Despite the long arm of the Spanish inquisition other islands such as Cuba and Puerto Rico also had settlements of Jews. In Latin America - Brazil, Mexico, Colombia and Argentina became home for many Jews. Some of these were *Crypto* or hidden Jews, residing in Spanish and Portuguese countries where they practiced in secret (Arbell, 2002). By the late 16th century, fully functioning Jewish communities were founded in the Portuguese colony of Brazil, the Dutch colonies of Suriname and Curaçao, Spanish colony of Santo Domingo, and the English colonies of Jamaica and Barbados. In addition, there were unorganized communities of Jews in Spanish and Portuguese territories where the Inquisition was active, including Colombia, Cuba, Puerto Rico, Mexico and Peru. Many of the members of these communities were also crypto-Jews, who had concealed their identity from the authorities, while worshipping in secret (Jewishwikipedia, www.jewishwikipedia.info/new_ world.html).

Suriname itself boasted the largest population of Jews. The "Dutch" as referenced in a number of historical works, were an important population for the development of the sugar industry in the Caribbean as well as trade and commerce within the Americas and across the Atlantic in Europe. While Santo Domingo and Cuba remained under Spanish rule, Jamaica passed from the hands of the Spanish to the British and Barbados remained in the hands of the British from the beginning. The colonial powers set up their trading posts and networks through the British and Dutch West India Companies, which were also to provide privateering contracts for the pirates in the Caribbean. Among them were several Jews who were known to carry out ritual prayers whilst pillaging in the open seas under their majesties protection (Kritzler, 2009). At the same time, the Jews coming to the Caribbean from Europe brought with them other cultural and religious customs such as the love of learning and the respect for worship. Werner states, "Study and worship went hand in hand; nay, study was worship and ignorance was a deadly sin" (Werner, 2015, p. 181).

FRENCH – HAITI

The year is 2010 and twenty-two of the twenty-three Haitian Jews left on the island, had already departed for the United States when Yuval Shomron briefly recorded his presentation of a gift to Joel Biggio, the last Haitian Jew. The story of the Jews on that island began with the arrival of the very first Jew to set foot in Santo Domingo, on the east of the land mass shared with Haiti on the west. He was Luis De Torres, who in 1492 accompanied Christopher Columbus on his maiden voyage, serving as an interpreter. The Jewish settlement in Haiti ends with Biggio, who was literally on his way to board a flight at the time of the brief encounter with Yuval (Shomron, 2010). So, the Jews arrived in Haiti and the adjoining Santo Domingo by ship and departed almost 500 years later by plane, after a sketchy and tumultuous stay on the twin island. The last record posted by Rabbi Lapin in 2014 attested to the absence of any Jewish community at that time.

> There are few or no Jews in Haiti. There is a sprinkling of itinerant Jews who work for the U.N. or the U.S. Embassy and myself and my son…Haiti has abundant fruits, vegetables and fish, all very inexpensive so keeping kosher here is not that great a challenge. The supermarkets carry American and French kosher products, although they are very expensive. We bring in meat and cheese from either Santo Domingo, New York or Miami. (Lapin, 2014)

The History of the Jews in Haiti has been a chequered one, perhaps as unsettled as the governance of that territory itself. The island is shared with another independent territory - Santo Domingo, which remained in the hands of the Spanish when the portion that is today known as Haiti, was taken over by the French in 1633. What transpires after this is a head-spinning series of events. One year later the Dutch Marrano Jews arrived, fleeing persecution in the Spanish colony of Brazil. But their time there was to be short-lived. By 1683 they were expelled from Haiti as well as the remaining French colonies, following the passing of the *Black Code* (Code Noir), restricting the activities of the negro population and the banning of all religions except Catholicism by Louis XIV. However, a small number of Jews continued to work for the French trading companies. Sephardic Jews from France joined the few Dutch traders in Haiti, settling in the south, with those fleeing Curacao settling in the north. The eighteenth century saw the return of some of the departed Jews, who were joined by a group of Polish Jews. Regrettably many perished during the slave revolts led by Toussaint Louverture (1791-1804). Over time the remaining numbers survived without any Jewish schools and education for the children, while operating covertly. It is estimated that by the end of the nineteenth century approximately thirty Sephardic Jewish families had arrived from Egypt and the Middle East.

Haiti again underwent further political turmoil when it was taken over by the United States in the early twentieth century. The population at the time had risen to approximated two hundred Jews. The presence of the U.S. in the island for two decades spurred another exodus of Jews to America. The issuing of Haitian passports to some three hundred Jews from Austria, Poland, Germany, Romania and Czechoslovakia saved these lives during the Holocaust, some not ever setting foot in the island, but benefitting from the opportunity the travel documents offered. Another exodus of Haitian Jews from the West Indies took place in the 1950s. The motivation this time was the search for other practicing Jews to marry. It appears throughout the Caribbean, men outnumbered women among the Jewish settlers. The same is true today of other islands. To avoid assimilation, the Jewish communities migrated to the United States, where they were more likely to find other Jews who had fled Europe and enjoy greater financial success as well. The U.S. and Panama, became chief destinations throughout the twentieth century for Jews from this island. The tombstones found in a number of Haiti's cities that have sea ports and the recent ruins of a synagogue in the city of Jeremie are the only archaeological reminders of the early Jewish presence on the island. At final count in 2013 the Jewish population fell to around twenty-five persons in the capital city of Port-au-Prince. Today, after Haiti's latest catastrophe of the 2016 hurricane Matthew, where the body count exceeded 1,000 (Delva, 2016) the Jewish community established in 1630 no longer exists. This is evidenced by Rabbi Lapin's earlier comment. No doubt however there are still some remaining descendants of assimilated Jews.

DUTCH - SURINAME AND CURAÇAO

Suriname's importance to Jewish life in the Caribbean lies in the fact that it not only has housed the largest group of settlers, but it has also provided a safe haven for Dutch Jews who have moved back and forth between the necklace of Caribbean islands, connecting them all to plantation life and the trade and commerce in the region during colonisation. Professor Norman Girvan places Suriname as part of the insular Caribbean (Girvan, 2005) although neither Suriname nor its neighbouring territory of Guyana are bordered by the Caribbean Sea. Its ties to the Caribbean are in its identity as a related territory with close relationships to the islands and goes beyond the issue of bordering waters and shared seas. Ideologically then, Suriname, Guyana and at times Belize are include in Caribbean socio-political relations and identification (Taglioni and Cruise, 2012). Our intent here is to demonstrate the linkages between them and the rest of the Jewish Caribbean and the history-making contribution of the Dutch Surinamese Jews to sugar production.

The World Jewish Congress places the settlement of Suriname by the Jews at 1635 – 1639 and puts their numbers at 2,000, which is said to be half the population of whites on the island. With the persecution of the Sephardic Jews in Portugal, during the inquisition, those who converted to Catholicism (Conversos) were aided in their flight from Europe by the gift of ships and safe passage by the king. They were intended to settle permanently in Brazil, but with continued persecution they moved towards the Guyanas and Suriname. The second wave of Dutch Jewish migration came during World War II, which created more refugees. The numbers of Dutch and other

European Ashkenazi Jews added to the existing Sephardim. Together they have maintained numbers upwards of 2,700 to this day. The Surinamese Jews hold the distinction of being the oldest community in the Americas (Juro, 2013).

Their successive synagogues date back to 1617 in Cassipora and attest to the vibrancy and longevity of the various communities. The Cassipora synagogue served the community until the end of the 18th century when they moved to the more prosperous area of Jodensavanne. Others included the *Bracha ve Shalom-Blessings and Peace*, built in 1685 was the Jodensavanne synagogue that eventually was overrun by the jungle after it had served the community for 100 years and preserved for another 80 years after it was no longer in use. The *Neve Shalom*-Oasis of Peace, was first built in 1719 by a community of Ashkenazis. It was renovated and expanded in the 1800's and is now the current synagogue in use by Ashkenazis and Sephardis who merged with the community in 1999, leaving behind their original place of worship - The *Zedek v Shalom-Justice and Peace*, built in 1735. Interestingly enough Suriname also boasted a Jewish mulatto and black community in Paramarimbo's *Darchei Yesharim-Way of the Righteous* synagogue, in the late 18th century. This synagogue was torn down in the 19th century and the community died out over the next three decades.

CURACAO

Since the arrival of Christopher Columbus in 1492 and the much later period culminating in the second world war of the 1940's, the Jewish exodus to the Caribbean has followed a similar pattern. It begins with the expulsion from Spain and Portugal into other parts of Europe and from there an exodus from Europe to the Caribbean, Latin America and later the United States. In Curacao, the first Jewish settlers arrived from the Netherlands around 1650. More than a century later, the Sephardic Jews built the *Mikve Israel Emanuel-Hope of Israel* synagogue in 1732 in Willemstad. The community has been there for close to 400 years and *Mikve Israel* has been in continuous use since its inception, serving the now 350 Jews. An interesting note on the practices of the Curacao community is their use of top hats during the Yom Kippur service, which is also seen in some congregations in England as noted by Schama (2016). This is another of the synagogues that in the Caribbean that has a sand floor. The others are in Kingston, Jamaica; Saint Thomas, US Virgin Islands; and Paramaribo, Suriname. The sand-floor tradition is one of the last remaining manifestations of Dutch-Portuguese Jewish life in this area. There are a number of theories put forward for the use of sand on the floors (Hakai Magazine, https://www.smithsonianmag.com/travel/Caribbean-synagogue-sand-floor-180963581/#yKPpAeB7j4bwy8Ul.99), which distinguishes these synagogues. Some say it is brought over from the Conversos who were worshipping in secret and the sand was meant to muffle the footsteps, others say it is a reminder of the long Exodus of the Jewish people in the desert (Schuessler, 2017, Repeating Islands, 2018). René Levy Maduro, in his late 70s and walking with a cane, spent four decades on the board of Mikvé Israel-Emanuel, and 15 of those as its President. He has watched the congregation change over the generations, but it is the attrition that is most concerning. Younger Jews are leaving the Caribbean in droves as they seek post-secondary education and other opportunities in the United States or Europe. The Ashkenazi Jews of Curacao built the *Shaarei Tsedek-Gates of Righteousness* synagogue in 1959 in Williamstad. The synagogue grew out of the earlier sports club that was founded in 1932. Despite the survival of the community to the present day and the relatively large numbers that they boast in their congregations, older members echo the concerns of many Caribbean communities, "We are on our way to extinction…Our numbers are just diminishing to the point of no return…Our numbers will just get smaller" (Podzkiewitz, 2007).

THE SPANISH - SANTO DOMINGO AND CUBA

On the North Coast of Santo Domingo (The Dominican Republic) lies a small Jewish settlement in the town of Sosua. The first 32 Jews to arrive in the island in 1938 were among the Jews of France who were fleeing persecution in Europe. The original agreement arrived at with the government of Santo Domingo was for the issue of 100,000 visas. Each year another group of 32 were to arrive but Germany did not hold up its end of the bargain and the small Ashkenazi community that first arrived, was later joined by Jews from other parts of Europe such as Luxemburg, Italy, Sweeden and others. Herbert Katz, an 86-year-old original member of the 32 settlers, speaks of his grandchildren and great grandchildren. As in the case of many settlers, he married a Dominican woman. The community is described by his grandson as progressive. In 1940 a further 686 Jews were given safe passage from Europe to Santo Domingo. The majority worked in agriculture and began farming and cheese production. In New York, the Dominican Republic Settlers Association oversaw the settlement of the immigrants to Santo Domingo. Joe Benjamin shared in his 2015 interview with Addis Burgos, that the current descendants were like one big family, and festivals and gatherings served as a reunion for sharing stories and photos from the past. In 1947 another group arrived from Shanghai, which had been their haven for a short time. As with other islands the Sosua community had members who left after the war for the USA and Canada.

The Jews of the Dominican Republic were the beneficiaries of a cruel twist of fate. In the period 1930 – 1961 the dictator Trujillo was in charge in Santo Domingo, and it was actually his deep racism against blacks that drove him to welcome the Jews of Europe. Each family was given a cow and a donkey to till the land. On the other hand, in Haiti Trujillo was to exterminate thousands of blacks (The Hidden Faith Project, 2011).

The present community of Sosua today has a synagogue-Centro Israelita de Republica Domincana, a cemetery and museum. Community Leader, Isaac Lalo, blames the dwindling community on intermarriage and migration.

CUBA

The years 1953-1959 in Cuba, saw the exodus of many of the remaining Jews. The revolution of 1959 not only changed the political directorate of this Caribbean island, but also created instability among the 15,000 Cryptos,

Marranos and Conversos in the country. Many of these Cuban Jews can be found in the Miami, Beth Shmuel Cuban-Hebrew Community (El Circulo). A group of over 400 "Operation Cigar" Jews slowly made their way to Israel.

Some of the early settlers were Conversos fleeing the Inquisition, though the largest numbers were Americans who arrived in 1902 seeking new business opportunities after the Spanish-American war and the independence of Cuba. They also set up the first synagogue-The United Hebrew Congregation of Cuba, and the first cemetery. The second wave of Jews were the Sephardim who came from Turkey and Syria in 1910. They set up their own organisation – the *Union Hebrea Chevet Ahim*. The next group of World War II refugees arrived, from eastern Europe and continued to arrive until the end of the war. They had intended to move on to the United States but remained in Cuba as restrictions were placed on migration to the US. During the period 1030-1950 the Jewish community grew and flourished, necessitating the organisation of the now, larger community with the establishment of the *Centro Israelita* Ashkenazi community centre. The Centro provided an organising hub for cultural, social and educational pursuits and soon established its own school. Zionist and Israeli social and political groups were also established to support the Jews in Palestine, and later the State of Israel. 1940-1959 Jewish commercial and social life enjoyed steady increase in prosperity. The *Patronato De La Casa de La Comunidad Hebreo de Cuba* centre was built in 1953. There was considerable intermarriage among the earliest settlers with the local population, resulting in considerable assimilation. The success of the Castro led Cuban Revolution was to sound the death knell for the once prosperous Cuban Jews. The new arrivals in Miami were generally given a wide berth by other Jews who entertained strong anti-Latino sentiment, with the exception of Rabbi Mayer Abramowitz of Temple Menorah, who was to become known as the Father of the Cuban Jews until his death at 97 years old (Miller, 2017, Weiner, https://www.jewishvirtuallibrary.org/cuba-virtual-jewish-history-tour).

Today it is estimated that some 1,000 Jews reside in Havana, with a further 500 scattered across the island (Gerszberg, 2007) coming from a community of some 20,000 Jews in the past. Since the recent liberalisation of the government dubbed, The Cuban Thaw", the remaining Jews have resumed services in Havana and Santiago de Cuba. The *Centro Sepharidi*, The Holocaust Museum and the *Beth Shalom-House of Peace* synagogue, are all in active use currently in Havana. Three other synagogues were built on the island: the Ashkenazi, *Shevet Ahim-Brothers Dwelling Together*, in the 1920's in Camaguey; The Sepharic synagogue of *Tiferet Israel-Beauty of Israel*, and the current Patronato, synagogue revived in the 1980's. Havana has had a total of 5 synagogues over time, a kosher restaurant and a Sunday school. Today the *Tikun olam - Heal the World,* school also instituted in the 1980's serves the community.

ENGLISH - BARBADOS AND JAMAICA

Barbados

Unlike the other English territories, Barbados was never in the hands of the Spanish. The English colonized the island in 1625 and the first Sephardic Jews arrived there three decades later from Brazil (Burns, 1954). Like other Jews at the time, they were fleeing the long arm of the inquisition that had reached across the Atlantic and Caribbean Seas into Latin America and the Caribbean. They brought with them the technology for sugar plantation and contributed to Barbados' wealth for more than a century after the establishment of the first plantations. Barbados thereby provides the first prototype for the production and export of sugar to Europe. This technology was exported to Jamaica and Santo Domingo where sugar flourished. Jews in Barbados as in the rest of the Caribbean, were restricted in their ownership of slaves and primarily made their wealth as merchants and traders. The first Jews left by the 1930s and the second wave, the Ashkenazis - arrived during the Second World War.

Bridgetown Barbados has two synagogues. The *Nidhe Israel-Scattered of Israel* Synagogue, originally built in 1654, has been restored along with a *mikveh-ritual bath*. It also houses a museum. The other synagogue is the *Shaare Tzedek-Gates of Justice*, they are used half year each. Barbados is among the Caribbean Jewish communities that has consistently made significant donations to Israel (Arbell, 2009). In 2015 the population numbered between 80 and 100 Jews (World Jewish Congress, http://www.worldjewishcongress.org/en/about/communities/BB).

Jamaica

The Jewish community in Jamaica this year marks some 363 years approximately since their arrival in the island. Their current synagogue, The Share Shalom is already more than a hundred years old and still is a hub of Jewish activity. The Jamaica Jewish Heritage Centre is located on the grounds of the Share Shalom and provides lectures and tours to visitors and local school populations. Teams of visitors participate in regular field trips to the island to restore and document the graves of the more than twenty burial sites that have been used by the congregations over time. Presently only two of the cemeteries are in use. The community has a school, Hillel Academy which extends from nursery grades to sixth form. Students come from all denominations locally and from overseas. The Jewish holidays are observed during the school year.

Five synagogues in total have been built on the small island of Jamaica as Jews settled across the island, rather than clustering in the capital or coastal towns. In 1692 the very first Portuguese synagogue in Port Royal was destroyed in the earthquake; following this in 1704 the *Neve Shalom-Oasis of Peace* synagogue was built in Spanish Town and the congregations migrated there. The *Sha'ar ha-Shomain-Gateway of the Valleys*, synagogue was built in 1744, while the Ashkenazi synagogue *Shaare Yasher-Gates of Blessing was* established in Kingston 1787 for the Anglo-German communities. Both synagogues were destroyed by fire in 1882 (Grater, 2016). The *Mikveh Israel-Hope of Israel*, Ashkenazi synagogue was established in 1796 and was in use until 1860. In Kingston the *Kahal Kadosh Shaar Shamaim-Holy Congregation of the Gates of Peace*, was constructed and later described as "most luxurious" (Andrade 1882, 48), unfortunately this synagogue was destroyed by fire in 1882. The present synagogue,

Shaarei Shalom-Gates of Peace, was rebuilt after all synagogues were destroyed in the massive earthquake of 1907. The earthquake was registered as 6.5 and was so powerful that all buildings in Kingston, the capital city suffered damage. The death toll was the greatest yet and tsunamis were reported along the coastal towns (Wilson, 2008, p. 70).

One of the early anthologies of the island of Jamaica by Fernando Henriques reports that the settlement of Jews in Jamaica was encouraged by the grandson of Christopher Columbus – Portugallo Colon, who was now the Marquis of Jamaica. "The Jews approached him, and he agreed to allow them to settle in 1530" (Henriques, 1957, p. 22). Later more Jews arrived on subsequent voyages as merchants and traders, and some even joined pirate communities in towns such as Port Royal in Jamaica, where they functioned as licensed pirates for the European crowns (Kritzler, 2009). Under British rule the Jews enjoyed freedom to practice their religious beliefs and enter into public service. By the 18th century the number of Jews in the island was at 1,000 and by the 19th century these numbers rose to more than 2,500. The Jews here were primarily merchants and enjoyed a level of freedom that was unprecedented. They served in parliament by 1831 and in 1849 Yom Kippur was celebrated by the closing of parliament. It is noted that approximately a quarter of all shops closed on Shabbat on a regular basis (Frank, 2004). The Jewish Jamaicans have made significant contributions to nation building including holding public office, creating and sustaining a shipping industry, the arts, education, media and manufacturing.

Although the numbers of Jews are reported to be some 200, the descendants of Jews are reported in the thousands both at home and abroad (Tortello, 2004). In times of economic and political unrest the Jews in Jamaica and the rest of the Caribbean have migrated to the United States and Canada. In fact, Jamaican Jews were instrumental in safeguarding the first Dutch Jews who were migrating to the then New Amsterdam (Arbell, 2009). American Historian and author of, "The Jewish Pirates of the Caribbean", Ed Kritzler, lived in Jamaica. He is quoted as saying, "It's all about survival…we are Jamaican Jews, we have a stake in this country and we were here before the English.' The United Congregation of Israelites as the congregation is called, is also a member of the Jewish Congregation of Latin

America and the Caribbean and the Commonwealth Jewish Council in London, as well as having an honorary consul to Israel, Mr. Ainsley Cohen Henriques. Jamaica retains close ties to Israel, and there are Israeli members of the congregation. Over the centuries of the life of the congregation there have been notable Rabbis, however in times of their absence David Stephen Cohen Henriques has served for close to 30 years on and off as Spiritual Leader.

THE ROLE OF THE JEWS IN THE CARIBBEAN

Wilfred S. Samuels (1936), in addressing the Jewish Historical Society of England noted that without an understanding of the role of the Jews in the British West Indies, there could be little understanding of the contribution of the Jews to Britain itself. At the time this may have seemed a rather curious claim to make, given that the life and commerce of the colonies was so far removed, literally and psychologically from that of the average sugar-consuming, rum-imbibing; tobacco-smoking, spice-eating Englishman. Samuels' paper was in response to the question, the British seemed to be posing at the time, "What have our Jews done for us?" His response was a thorough documentation of the transatlantic trade and profits derived by Britain from its territories in the West Indies. It is a veritable historian's dream, as it lists the contribution to that document of every functionary and lay person in the Caribbean and Britain. Each new thread mentioned by Samuels, reveals a host of new information that is beyond the scope of this present psycho-social analysis of identity.

> I have formed the impression that our Colonial Jews rendered more pronounced services to the realm in the British West Indies than in any other part. Moreover, some knowledge of British "West Indian matters seems to me to be absolutely essential for a proper understanding of the seventeenth and eighteenth-century history of the London Sephardi community, since its members appear to have derived so much of their

social prestige—and so much of their revenue—from their Caribbean connections (Samuels, 1680, 2).

The presence of the Jews in the Caribbean in the early years of their settlement, and in more recent times, has been one that transformed over the years through necessity and later in pursuit of prosperity. Perhaps the first of the merchant class in the Caribbean, the Jews traded sugar, tea, coffee tobacco, grain and gold. Under the guise of Conversos – newly converted Christians – they continued undisturbed for long periods of time (Ketzler, 2009). During the period from the end of the 16th century into the greater part of the 17th century there were some Jews who took to the seas and enjoyed some notoriety among the Buccaneers of the Caribbean. Kritzler himself documents the exploits of these dangerous men, such as the infamous and feared Sinan Barbarossa and the Pirate Rabbi Samuel Palache along with Motta the Portuguese. These seafaring robbers, not only worked as independents but also were for hire by the crown. They formed an itinerate fleet that often relieved vessels plying their way to Europe, of their valuable goods. Some of the profits realised during periods of "privateering" were taxed by the various governments, chief among them was Britain. In this way the pirates benefitted, and the crown exercised its right to tax them through their bounty (Kritzler, 2009).

As it relates to the trade in slaves there are mixed views on the extent to which Caribbean Jews actually took part in the trade. Those who are kind to the history of the Jews, point out the restrictions placed on them, which barred them from owning large numbers of slaves (Bennett, sefarad.org). Others document the Jewish trade between the American mainland and Africa in slaves, as well as the supply of ships for the trade. What is certain is the instrumental role played by the Jews in the infrastructure and engineering of the sugar production. Sugar became one of the first crops to arrive in Britain as a finished product, ready for sale. Rum was also favoured both as an export product as a means of payment. Both derived from the sugar cane grown on the plantations. The contribution of sugar and rum to the British economy cannot be overstated as the proceeds from the West Indies brought in enough capital to build two towns and supplement the gross national product of Britain. Sugar production heralded the birth of the factory and the start of the industrial age in the United Kingdom. There is some debate in the more recent literature as to the role of Jews in plantation life as they owned very few estates but provided ample technical and financial skill in the trade of goods across the Atlantic. Most academic sources covering slavery agree that the Shabbat and Kosher household customs, along with the legal prohibition in most of the islands against Jews owning more than one or two slaves, would have been sufficient to exclude them from the large-scale ownership of slaves. Their interests and financial advancement came about in large part due to the vast networks of Iberian diaspora Jews to be found throughout the trading posts and cities of Europe, and their relatives now scattered across the Caribbean. Corporations designed for trade and commerce had already been set up by the colonial powers to organize and profit from the trade in slaves from Africa, goods from the Caribbean and supplies from Europe. This three-way trade allowed for a larger labour force to be brought from Africa as slaves, to work on the plantations of the Caribbean. They produced rare spices and food products that would grace the households of Europe in exchange for linens and other necessary supplies. Their greatest asset being what Jane Gerber refers to as having, "…a cousin in every port", which allowed them to exchange goods and services globally (Shalom TV, 2013). But without the ability to trade safely from one side of the known world to the other by sea, the wealth of Europe was at the mercy of the pirates and profiteers, waiting to relieve the traders of their hard-earned goods and cash. The dispersed Iberian Jews invented international banking through the use of promissory notes that could be safely carried across the perilous seas of the Atlantic, instead of gold or silver coins. These could later be exchanged thousands of miles away in Europe (Sombart, 2015). The tragedy of Jewish persecution and expulsion from Europe had slowly been transformed into the triumph of global trade, engineering and banking. Jews became merchants and traders, bankers and engineers. Ironically, the very status of Sephardic Jews as, "not quite white" allowed them to be, …positioned in the colonial enterprise as "the international cross-cultural brokers par excellence" (Sutcliffe, 2016 in Phillips Casteel), serving as navigators, translators, and traders who facilitated the conquest of the New World, where they also introduced agricultural techniques that helped to develop the plantation economy (Phillips Casteel, 2016). The infrastructure for the sugar plantations, which began in Barbados, would not have been possible without the work of the Dutch Jews. The initial work force of poor, Irish Whites was soon worn out and insufficient in numbers. The arrival of African slaves allowed for the expansion of the prototype model of the plantation "factory" from Barbados to Jamaica and other Caribbean islands. In those islands where Spain and France had been ousted by the Dutch and English, Jews enjoyed relative freedom and therefore prosperity. Their innovative letters of exchange and credit made capital portable. For instance, a shipping merchant trading in pirate waters doubled his risks if he returned with gold. On the other hand, if he could leave the gold and return instead with a draft on a Jewish banking house, he was safe. As a link in a world trade network at the onset of international trade, Jewish merchants were the world's most coveted capitalists. (Kritzler, 2009, p. 5).

The story of the Caribbean Jew is one of survival by assimilation, adaptation and filling the gaps where obstacles to prosperity existed. Departure, migration, mobility, travel and the resilience to re-invent oneself while holding fast to a central identity, is at the core of Jewish life (Gerber, 2013). Survival throughout time and across nations has been predicated on the ability to adapt, not give up, Jews appear to have developed a sort of psychological evolution towards preservation. While this same tenacity may be true of other tribes, the Jew has been destroyed and resuscitated many times, on many more continents, and still the fierce communism and sense of belonging to each other, has been their greatest psychological tool. Austrian neurologist and psychotherapist Viktor Frankl, who survived the Nazi concentration camps at Auschwitz, reasons that survival depends on the ability to accept the psychological tension between what is happening to you in this very moment - however horrible - and what you will become in the future when this moment passes. For Frankl, "Such a tension is inherent in the human being and therefore is indispensable to mental well-being. We should not, then, be hesitant about challenging man with a potential meaning for him to fulfill" (Frankl, 2006, p. 106). The decision to accept the realities in front of us, while balancing the possibilities that hope for the future contains, is essential to psychological survival. This recognition of the importance of seeing a thing for what it is and accepting that things can indeed be different in the future, is a vital quality of good psychotherapy. Without this ability to manage the polarities between despair and its polar opposite, our self-efficacy and self-esteem suffers and ultimately our will to be masters of our own lives too. For Jews everywhere the expression, *"never forget"*, can be understood as an exaltation to see things as they are, as they have been and still look to the future. It is part of the Jewish psyche, that holds on to the mental image of the candle lit in the dark, to bring hope. In the next chapter we take a look at how identity is formed and reaffirmed throughout the lifespan, and the meaning of all this for our self-concept.

Chapter 2

JEWISH IDENTITY

I arrived early to attend a Shabbat service in a Caribbean synagogue, siddur-prayer book in hand. As I sat down at the end of the row, near the entrance, I was approached by an older man. He greeted me cordially and quickly went on to ask, "Do you have lineage?" It seemed a somewhat awkward way to greet a stranger, but frankly I have become used to the guarded, curiosity that Caribbean Jews demonstrate towards others. I open my siddur and point to a name in the Acknowledgements page. He nods, smiles, bows slightly and says, "Shalom". As he walks toward the door to greet another stranger I realise that his yamulka-skull cap atop the white shock of hair, blue and white prayer shawl over his white shirt, black pants, and the long, full grey beard make him look like a flashback from the past.

A PERSONAL PSYCHOLOGY AND PHILOSOPHY OF IDENTITY

At this juncture I want to take a therapeutic look at the identity issue and start by saying that those who struggle with the ambiguities of multiple cultural identities can fully comprehend the importance of identity politics in the community and the world. They sometimes feel they have betrayed themselves and others by leaving out some aspect of their identity that may not be apparent to others. The proverbial 'passing' because they have been raised within the framework of a cultural identity which is now so ingrained in their way of being. The act of claiming a set of identities that you feel emotionally and culturally connected to in everyday life is part of our self-definition. However, it can also be a double-edged sword to be able to claim one identity over another, depending on your circumstances and geographic location. When we assert a particular set of cultural identities we immediately run the risk of offending those who feel betrayed by their exclusion from these categories, as well as those who feel violated by your inclusion within their sacred cultural walls. In my professional role as a psychologist, I am often asked by clients seeking to make better romantic and life choices, 'What did I do wrong? How can I choose better?' My answer usually centre's around two basic elements of their life worlds: 1) their personal psychology 2) their personal philosophy. These may seem like odd categories and anything but personal, but if you will allow me a small digression I will attempt to demonstrate why these are important and how they contribute to a solid sense of identity.

I think of therapy as a means of arriving at clarity about ourselves, our intentions and our relationships with others and also for helping us to face the reality of our lives. I remind my clients often of what our joint goal is during the process, that is to achieve clarity and face reality. It follows therefore that if we are to gain any degree of clarity we must experience some insight into what ails us, and what we want to do about it. This is what I consider the personal psychology. Outside of any theoretical approaches that I might bring to the session, if the client is unwilling to see their situation as entirely in their hands, and the interpretation of same as their own perspective, that might not be shared by others in the very situation, then there is little progress that can be made. In accepting that we have a personal motivation to correct the errors in our own lives, to remedy the problems of which we are a part and to accept that some of what we have co-created is unpleasant and undesirable, then we begin to make progress toward an understanding of our own personal psychology.

Second, having grasped our own agency in the life we create for ourselves we now have a more fundamental and far-reaching task, that of creating a new paradigm, a new framework that incorporates our present state of clarity and reality. We are now tasked with developing a personal philosophy for how we will move forward and take agency over our life world. Our personal psychology speaks to what we intend in our lives, our motivations and the ideal state that we are searching for, while our personal philosophy speaks to the framework we use in interpreting life's challenges and accomplishments. It informs how we accept the experiences that we share in. The framework, the lens or paradigm that we use to make meaning of our lives will naturally colour our experiences, making us view them as positive or negative, helpful or harmful. Whether our philosophy is based in religious practice, be it Christian, Jewish, Buddhist, Muslim or secular precepts, the response to our lived experiences are informed by that philosophy.

With clients I often ask them to imagine the future they would like to have, rather than the events and beliefs that led them to a place of crisis. The person, they want to be can usually be summed up in very few words, and if they have a clear vision of someone who embodies what they want, they are that much closer to achieving this sense of self. Usually there is a word, or set of words, a metaphor that speaks to what they want for themselves in the future. All this work is impossible without developing a clear sense of individual identity, as we work through the issues toward a psychology and philosophy of your own. Identity is the key that unlocks our unique and personal journey with our integrity and the reputation we will gain with ourselves.

The tendency generally is for individuals to accept what we are told, what we are given and not to question whether we believe the traditions that are handed down to us without interrogating them. The average person is startled by the idea that they could develop a personal philosophy because they see it as such an awesome task and something for great thinkers. Yet it starts with understanding our own motivations and core principles. It starts with the simple, most often asked question of the human experience, 'Who am I and what am I here to accomplish?' It starts with an act of identity.

> The purpose of philosophy is to provide man with an integrated view of existence, of his own nature, and of his relationship to the world in which he lives. Philosophy is the science that deals with man's relationship to existence. (Branden, 2009, paragraph 2, Kindle location 225 of 999)

Philosophy as the science of man's relationship with the world, presents us with infinite choices as to how we will challenge or accept the traditions that came before us. Even as we accept what has served generations in the past, because tradition has great value, there is still the need to recognize that ultimately the identities we claim is a choice. One that is both an internal conviction of who we will show up as to ourselves, and an external manifestation of who we ask the rest of the world to accept us as. It is us asking others to see us as we see ourselves, it is a dialogue within ourselves and with others.

IDENTITY AND THE SELVES

When we speak of identity we generally refer to the unifying whole that a person presents to the outside world, because of the beliefs they hold about themself. The psychological self can also be understood as twofold, the presenting self and the real self. If we imagine that each of the selves is a kind of metaphorical container for things that we believe and demonstrate to the world about ourselves, we might easily distinguish between the two selves. The first, *the perceived self*, contains the beliefs we have about our own characteristics, such as being clever, handsome, pretty, chubby, astute, talented, witty, humorous, tall, thin, short, likeable and many more. We place in the *perceived self*, container, those attributes that we want others to recognise us by, our ideal, private notions of ourselves, even if we don't possess those attributes. Our *presenting self* contains those behaviours and attitudes that we demonstrate to the world. It is how others experience us, it is our public self. The social context, the culture, the physical and social environment mediates between the perceived and presenting selves, making us aware of what is permitted, acceptable and desirable (Allport, 1961, Adler and Proctor II, 2010). Society in general, and our smaller social groups to which we belong reward and punish us depending on the public self that we display to them. We depend on their approval to know where we stand in relationships. However, identity is a tricky business and actually requires a degree of non-conformity, to assert ourselves and to demand that we be treated according to our inner, private notions of ourselves. This brings about the integrity of character required to really confront the world as autonomous, self-sufficient adults worthy of respect. It is the tension that exists between the perceived self's need to assert itself and the presenting self's need to adhere to social ideals. Balancing both these tensions brings about the real self, the person we truly are. The process of defining the identity that we will claim for ourselves starts as early as two years, with our first "No" and continues through different challenges throughout the lifespan. It continues into adolescence where the accumulated socialisation, challenges and triumphs of our life experiences become integrated, as the ego battles with itself and the world outside, for true definition. It is no wonder then that universally throughout the world we have sought to bring adolescents into adulthood using various rites of passage, whether it be added responsibilities, celebrations or religious rituals. It is at this point that the ego integrity of the self becomes defined and finds its purpose in the larger society. We begin to feel that we know who we are, who we are meant to be and how we would like to be experienced by those around us. Our struggle for ego autonomy, brings us into contact with our real selves. In the words of psychologist Erik Erikson, "In the social jungle of human existence, there is no feeling of being alive without a sense of identity" (Erikson, 1980, p. 95). When we can define our ego identity, our concept of self, we can recognize our individual purpose and truly experience ourselves as alive. Further if we are truly alive then we must act in the world, and this action is a cumulative effect of the ways in which we have identified ourselves, and the external expressions of those identifications over the years. To say I am a Jew, means to be alive as a Jew and to express that private and public self in ways that integrate my sense of a Jewish identity. However, Jewish is not all that I am, so I am also forced to examine my other identifications and to integrate those as well into my self-schema.

IDENTIFICATION

For the purposes of this conversation I would also like us to consider the many ways in which others label and identify us. The term *identification* is used here in the social sense of the labels others assign to us. These labels are restricted to the categories know by the others, those external phenotype characteristics that we equate with race and ethnicity. Identification parades, as used in the criminal sense, seek to single out the suspect in relation to a crime. It also seems in many instances that multi-ethnic persons are suspected of the crime of racial ambiguity. They create confusion for those who need neat little boxes to reduce the complexity of straddling more than one category of cultural expression. The individual, on the other hand, may well incorporate this liminality within their cultural/ethnic/racial schema and have little difficulty managing these polarities and the spaces in between. The problem then is a social one. The '*others*' need to identify, which of the suspected stereotypes may be applied to the individual, so they can sleep comfortably at night. The ambiguity nags at them as if they think you are hiding behind the obvious features of your phenotype characteristics such as skin colour, hair, eyes. Language, speech and dress may also play a role in this identification because these visible cues support a social expectation that the individual will live up to the identification labels placed on them. If you are identified within your culture as Black, White, Chinese or Indian, Jewish, those around you have an expectation of how you will speak, dress, eat and live. In cultures where there are mostly related or homogenous groups of people, whoever expresses distinct and separate visible minority status is subjected to a form of hyper-scrutiny of *identification*. The Black-ness, White-ness, Chinese-ness, and Indian-ness, Jewish-ness appears to be more pronounced and serves to create division and exclusion. As Freud put it, we become involved in a form of '*narcissism in respect of minor differences*'.

> I once interested myself in the peculiar fact that peoples whose territories are adjacent, and are otherwise closely related, are always at feud with and ridiculing each other, as for instance, the Spaniards and the Portuguese, the North and South Germans, the English and the Scotch, and so on. I gave it the name of narcissism in respect of minor differences...One can now see that it is a convenient and relatively harmless form of satisfaction for aggressive tendencies, through which cohesion amongst the members of a group is made easier. (Freud, 1929, p. 26).

It is almost as if the very proximity of the Other is what provokes the obsession on differences. Freud goes on to say that all the persecutions of the Jews in Europe has not benefitted their persecutors in their attempt to eradicate them. Sander Gilman in her work, Freud, Race and Gender, says, "For Freud in the 1870s the idea of race is a confining, limiting factor, as it implies a biological, immutable pattern of development" (Gilman in Magonet, 1995, p. 136). This obsession with dissecting small differences and deviations from social stereotypes and biological identity, in my view belongs to the category of voices I will call the *ethnicists*. For them identity is a biological, ethnic, even racial fact and not an inter-psychic self-assertion. It is important to note that while Freud adhered to the notion of a Jewish psyche, and increasingly so after the war and his own exile, he rejected the *ethnicist* position that Jewish identity could be determined by biological and racial differences. At the same time, he asserts, particularly in his personal communications, that there is a special way of thinking that is distinctly Jewish.

THE ROLE OF THE OTHER

Existentially, the role of the other in our understanding of our identities is so that we can have a mirror held up to the presenting self, who performs what Goffman refers to as the "frontstage behaviour" (1956). When we encounter *the other*, our presented-self collides with the image reflected back at us from *the others,* an image that may not be in sync with our private image of ourselves. In a sense, others keep us honest about who we say we are, and who we are seen as, in the social context. In the words of Jean Paul Sartre, "The other is indispensable to my existence, and equally so to any knowledge I can have of myself" (1946, p. 3). Essentially the other person helps us to define ourselves. The interplay between the selves is a lifelong, gradual process that helps us to cement a self-concept. We try to live up to the image we have of ourselves privately and socially. Failure to do so in many cases results in a kind of identity fraud, a pseudo-identity is developed, to present the self to the world in ways that are consistent with the idea we have of ourselves. This counterfeit self cannot be sustained without considerable difficulties and psychological injury. The psychoses and cognitive/emotional dissonance that result often lead to a breakdown in the personality. Hiding from ones' identity or appropriating an identity that is counterfeit, produces the same results. To suppress any part of the individual identity, to deny ones' personal autonomy in that assertion, is to ask the psyche to believe a lie. Equally, to ask Caribbean natives to choose between Jewish mother or father and gentile parent along with the inherited identities that may be entailed in that intermarriage is to suggest psychological genocide.

HYPHENATED REALITIES

The answer to the Jewish identity question, for the most part throughout the Caribbean has been a pragmatism of accepting intermarriages and multi-ethnic children into the congregations. In truth our identity is not one single thing. There is no real dichotomy between being Jewish and being Caribbean, but rather we occupy the many categories simultaneously. We experience ourselves as a hyphenated reality, as many things at the same time. We are multi-racial, multi-ethnic, Jewish-Caribbean men and women. I invite us to consider the notion of hyphenation rather than the idea of hybridity, which suggests a biological re-engineering of the identity of two different species. The hyphen is used as a means of combining meaning to create a whole, that is greater than its constituent parts. The same is true of the many ethnicities that come together in any group of Jewish descendants in the islands.

Elsewhere, in countries that receive large numbers of migrants, such as Britain, the United States, and Canada. Hyphenation has become more than a grammatical term, it signals issues of identity for migrant populations. Immigrants entering these countries are now encouraged to embrace all of their ethnic and geographic identities. However, for some especially in Britain this has created a new contention. In the United States, scholar Berel Lang, author of 34 books, looks at the issue of hyphenation and Jewish anxiety first from the viewpoint we have taken here, as in the grammatical signifier, and then as it relates to the notional melting pot of the United States culture and ideology. In his work, *Hyphenated Jews and the Problem of Anxiety* (2005), he sets out to challenge the nationalist view that the American psyche has no room for hyphenated Americans, as Presidents Roosevelt and Wilson are purported to have said. Lang is concerned with, "…the syntax of "hyphenated-Jews", and how such individuals are characterized in the American-Jewish and other Jewish Diaspora communities. The hyphen also shapes,' Israeli-Jewish identity and, arguably, Jewish identity as such" (Lang, 2005, p. 2). It is a provocative read, which lays bare the issues of integration and otherness. The desire to maintain an identity as the place I am coming from, and another as the place I have landed in, and further the ability to choose which to embody at any given moment. Just as in the countries of migration the issue of identity signals issues of allegiance, there is the sense in the Caribbean among the majority Afro-Caribbean population that hyphenated Caribbean minorities are always one foot in and one foot out of national belonging at all times. I doubt that this notion represents any psychological truth, as it is possible to be both and then some. No one part of an identity is always in ascendance and when it comes to culture, habits, and rituals of daily life it is probably more difficult to untie the strands of the common rope that bind them together than to untangle the hyphenated self. The same is true of the psychological experience of multi-ethnicity.

In the 21st century the Caribbean person is more likely than ever to straddle multiple ethnicities, naturally the descendants of the original

Sephardim are among these hyphenated persons. The islands are comprised of Persian-European-Jews, Sephardic-Indo-Caribbean-Jews, Ashkenazi-Dutch-Caribbean-Jews, Chinese-Caribbean-Sephardic-Jews, European-Ashkenazi-Multi-ethnic-Jews. The history books of the region that have been used for many decades attest to the unique nature of Caribbean culture pointing out that it is the history of all "The People Who Came" (Brathwaite, 1968) from Europe, Africa, China and India combined. The issue of identity is not just about ethnicity however, and ethnicity is not just about our phenotype characteristics, it is also about who we can acceptably and reasonable cross the borders of identity with. We imagine the permissions and penalties of betraying family, the social and cultural norms we will violate when we choose to love outside the safe lines of tradition. Such decisions are often driven by passion and romantic love, and less often by logical reasoning. The thinking around interethnic, interfaith unions has advanced somewhat, and there have always been examples of small percentages of unions that deviate from traditional, within-ethnicity unions. In the United States there is an estimated eight percent of marriages that cross boundaries of faith and culture (Yodanis, Lauer and Risako, 2012). The traditional view is that the attraction between cultures is the final frontier between maintaining ones ethnic and cultural separateness and the breakdown of same.

> Intermarriage is generally regarded as a litmus test of assimilation. A high rate of intermarriage signals that the social distance between the groups involved is small and that individuals of putatively different ethnic backgrounds no longer perceive social and cultural differences significant enough to create a barrier to long-term union. (Alba and Nee, 2003, 90).

More recent studies (Batson, Qian, & Lichter, 2006) suggest that it is the erasure of the perceived differences between potential lovers that results in assimilation through marriage. Other research shows that cross ethnic relationships can actually be born out of an attraction to the ethnic, cultural and religious differences of the potential partner. Couples who are attracted to each other's differences are referred to as, "Affiliative ethnics [who] are drawn to an ethnic identity that is unrelated to their own ethnic ancestry and are motivated to deepen their knowledge, consumption, and enactment of that ethnic culture (Jimenez, 2010, p. 3). Engaging in an interethnic romantic relationship is a particularly important way to enact an affiliative ethnic identity. Yet another perspective is furthered by Daryll Bem, which suggest that we are sexually attracted to the unknown in each other, that is, the exotic. Our attraction to the unfamiliar becomes sexually appealing and exotic. Bem's EBE (exotic becomes erotic) theory, "…provides a single, unitary explanation for both opposite-sex and same-sex desire - and for both men and women" (2012, 532). We can easily see from Bem's perspective how the exotic of the "foreigner" could translate into the "erotic" pull across the rigid boundaries of interethnic, sexual and romantic pleasure.

SEXUAL IDENTITY

How we think of ourselves as it relates to who we are attracted to, constitutes our sexual orientation (hetero, homo, pan or queer), while the gender we are socialised into (masculine or feminine) and the biological sex (male or female) each contribute to how we identify sexually. For some these four categories of orientation, gender, biology and identity are aligned in traditional and majority expressions of sexuality, such as heterosexual, masculine, boy who sees himself as defined sexually by sexual relationships with women. Others may self-identify and express themselves sexually as a combination of any of the other categories mentioned above. More importantly however, is the interaction between our private sexual self and the social dictates that the public places on us as members of distinct cultural groups. We are not only seen as our private sexual selves by our partners, but society also places on us certain sexual expectations according to our perceived cultural groups. Whichever continent an individual derives from, Africa, the Americas, Asia, Australia, Europe, there are distinct perceptions about our sexual appetites, preferences and sexual appeal. These stereotypes for sexual behaviour are also placed on nationalities and specific groups within a country. We use these social stereotypes to inform our choices partly because they provide a shortcut to understanding behaviour, even when they are incorrect and also because they are cognitively efficient. If we think of the characteristics of a group, and project those onto an individual member of that ethnic/cultural group, we can shortcut all the tiny decisions we would otherwise have to make before deciding if they are a suitable romantic partner. We sexually stereotype different cultural groups as aggressive, sexy, lustful, charming, unfaithful. However, sexual stereotypes can also be disarming when a particular ethnic group is stereotyped as harmless, non-sexual, chaste and ineffectual as Jewish men have often been viewed. "More often than not, Jewish men on TV are brainy and sharp-witted; however, they can also be clumsy and awkward, both socially and physically. Even the appealing Ross on Friends is a wimp, and Seinfeld's pseudo-Jewish George, schlemiel extraordinaire, is the show's perennial loser" (Antler, https://www.myjewishlearning.com/article/gender-stereotypes-in-television/). The developmental crises of identity faced in adolescence by Jewish youth has been described by Lasser (1994) as one in which the teen wants to feel as athletic as his Black peers, but recognises that he will never be the jock, so he doesn't compete on this scale. The young man must resolve his identity issues by claiming that intellectual space that is reserved for him and where he is stereotypically likely to excel. "Socialized to study rather than play football, the Jewish adolescent stands outside of the mainstream masculine image...Whereas other racial, ethnic groups may use athletic ability as a demarcation of adult masculinity, Jews rely upon intellectual skills" (Lasser, 1994, 3-4). This kind of sexual stereotype puts the Jewish man at least, outside the possibility of sexual transgression and neutralizes his libido. Professor of Yiddish Studies, Jessica Kirzane (2004), examines the Jewish male and his encounters with women deemed taboo, through Yiddish American literary tropes. In her chapter titled, "What Kind of Man are You?", she makes the point that the sense of "Jewish difference" is not something that is only experienced by non-Jews, but also by Jews themselves who understood their Jewishness as something that sets them apart (Kirzane in Grushcow, 2004, p195). This is essentially what identity speaks to. It is not the ways in which others identify us or label us, it is the ways in which we claim aspects of our hyphenated selves. Krizane looks at what she calls the *interethnic* sexual encounters as a way of peeling back the layers on Jewish male sexuality. An important factor in the process of survival and assimilation in a Caribbean context where few Jewish women are available, and where the stereotypes of the lusty Black and Creole woman is inviting. In Glozman's "In the Fields of Georgia" the wandering Jewish salesman is unable to consummate his sexual desire for the fleshy negress because of his commitments to his wife far away and because of his own self-control. In Bashevis Singer's "The Slave", when the male protagonist, who has been sold as a slave, crosses the boundaries of his Jewish sexual identity with a Polish woman, disaster inevitably follows. It is the struggle between passion and sexual restraint that the novel plays with, demonstrating that the former is a central value of Jewish identity. The final of the three Yiddish novels, "New Yorkish" by Shapiro, describes an encounter between a Jewish man and a Latin American prostitute in New York. The seduction by the prostitute and surrender of the Jew, transforms the act into a pseudo marital encounter and the male protagonist is surprised by the tenderness he experiences although he is buying love. Krizane points out that in all three works the Jew has to encounter himself as on the fringes of society, like the Black woman-susceptible to forbidden love; like the Polish woman-unable to resist temptation and avoid disaster; and like the Latina, existing in a racially-ambiguous space. Krizane compares these encounters with the reflection of the fluid identity of the male protagonists with the stereotype social expectation of them. The protagonists are anchored by the knowledge and surety of their Jewishness. "The Jewish men in these stories crave the comfort of racial belonging, of homeland, of sexual pleasure and release, but find themselves…in a position of in-betweenness…" (Kirzane, 2004, 207).

Transgressions take many forms. The betrayals that accompany them include the betrayals of the self-identity, our integrity and the opinions that we hold of our perceived self. Our self-esteem is reflected in the people we engage with sexually, whether the encounters be brief or over a lifetime (Branden, 1980). That reflected appraisal of the other, reminds us of how far, or how close we have to come to reflecting our sexual selves in our partners, and this goes beyond ethnicity, religion and culture. The encounter allows you to see parts of yourself in very intimate contexts. Who you want to be when you engage in a sexual encounter is important to the enjoyment of that encounter. We seek out partners that will allow us to experience ourselves, as we see ourselves, to give us visibility. "There is the need to be loved and to feel visible. There is the need of self-discovery. There is the need of sexual fulfilment. There is the need of fully experiencing oneself as a man or as a woman" (Branden, 2008, p81-82). Sex is an essential part of the expression of identity, it is the vital link to the future, it is a private act, guided by the public taboos and dictates of cultural norms. In Phillip Roth's, "Human Stain" the biracial character - Coleman Silk – provides another example of an ambiguous ethnic identity. The protagonist is a university professor who has passed as Jewish for the better part of 50 years. Only when he is charged with racial discrimination against another minority, do we see his real identity revealed through the slow dismantling of his Jewish pseudo-identity. The protagonist plays into the ethnic stereotype of his times by assuming the presenting self that is neither White nor Black, but believable ambiguous, he adopts the cloak of a Jew, and denounces his family to maintain the fraud. He plays into the social stereotypes of the intellectual Jew and is believed due in part, to the racial stereotypes society holds of Jews. Since all behaviour takes place within a context, the social backdrop of culture will tell us what acts of identity it supports for particular ethnic groups, and which acts must remain underground.

CULTURE

Culture is concerned with those cohesive forces that pull us towards a common purpose, a sustaining system of belief, the preservation of a way of life. Archaeologist L. R. Binford describes culture as systems of human organisation that include, "…technologies and modes of economic organization, settlement patterns, modes of social grouping and political organization, religious beliefs and practices, and so on" (Binford, 1968, p.323). To understand the currents that run throughout Caribbean culture, and unite a seemingly disparate group of people, who are neither indigenous to the islands they inhabit, nor who have come to live on those islands voluntarily, it is important to understand the psyche of these hyphenated people and their worldviews. Some of the common beliefs that have permeated Caribbean society as it relates to colour/race and ethnicity, include the *colour bar*, which rewards phenotype characteristics that move furthest away from the Black, Indian, Chinese ideal and yet avoid the absolute alienation that Whiteness would convey. This stratification of colour, used in the period of slavery for the sale of slaves into various occupational categories, begins with Black at the base and continues in an ascending order to Sambo, Mullatto, Mustee, Mustiphini, Quintaroon, Octoroon, Free Coloured, culminating in the apex – White (Smith, 1965, Henriques, 1957). Vestiges of the slave psyche are still to be seen in some territories of the region, which value highly stratified societal rules that maintain what Smith refers to as the plural society maintaining its divisions while living alongside each other. Caribbean culture, if we can claim such a thing, celebrates hybridity, mélange and hyphenation as strength. It rewards the ambiguity of the supposed "mixed race" individual who can straddle a variety of realities and contexts. It is seen even today in the islands where there has been a large number of African slaves in the past, the current female ideal is not the White ideal, but rather the affirmed, in-between, brown skinned, curly hair mixture that is neither Black nor White. A form of creolized outsider, made legitimate by the extent to which they have allowed integration and assimilation. Simon Clarke (2008) positions culture and identity as essentially a discussion of differences. He contends that previous, well-reasoned arguments such as that of Foucault and Goffman, while concretizing the elements of performance and self-determination, do not take into account the questions of imagination and emotions in the consideration of identity formation. As a sociologist he recognises the missing link in the identity discussion to be the psycho-dynamic, "…the human imagination and emotion – the way in which people imagine the world to be and imagine the ways that others exist in the world …" (Clarke, 2008, p. 511). Goffman on the other hand, is not concerned with the individual ego-identity and therefore ignores motivation or intentionality on the part of the individual. If we exclusively employ a social psychology or sociology frame in analyzing identity we lose sight of the essential elements that make us uniquely human, such as the emotional, cognitive and motivational factors. Instead we reduce individual self-concept to the realm of herd mentality, teams and group-think. Motivation is what determined who partners bore children with and imagination is what led them to foresee the possibility of the creole offspring. In the Caribbean the act of *putting a little milk in your coffee*, afforded clear benefits to the mixed-race offspring who would be moved further from the field and closer to the great house, in slave society. The status of Creole confers social and economic gains to the individual. The emotional distance from the Black and White categories could be manipulated to the advantage of the individual. This still holds true to a large degree in Caribbean society.

CREOLISATION

Caribbean identity occurs within the discursive space of the "Creole". To be, "Caribbean" is to be "creolised" and within this space are accommodated all who, at any one time, constitute a (semi) -permanent core of Caribbean society…Everyone located in this discursive space, whatever her/his diasporic origin, becomes transformed in a regime of identical solidarity" (Hintzen, 2002, p. 92). This postcolonial discourse around race, colour, ethnicity and intermarriage, is essentially a conversation about power and how power has been distributed among the inhabitants of the former colonies. These power strictures have persisted, if not in everyday practice, certainly in the psyche of the individuals who are governed by them. The very advantages that were once awarded the ambiguous other, have now become suspect in the last 30 years as political rhetoric in the Caribbean has become about Blackness and declared nationalism. Cultural identity theorist, Stuart Hall, in speaking of his own Jamaica, asserts that the notion of Blackness was something not spoken about in his childhood. It was something hidden, that did not get a public – political voice until after the Black Power movement around the Caribbean (Hall, 2017). He argues that Blackness did not enter the public vocabulary, nor was it thought of as positive until after the movement of the 1930s. The term "creole" which has been borrowed from the French, originally indicated a Black-European (French) mix but has come to signify mixture between Black and many other groups in the region. Those who occupy the space in-between Blackness and Whiteness have become foreigners in their new home, once again. This necessitates an active psychological suppression and denial of difference for the Caribbean individuals who are identified as being from minority groups. They become perceived as foreign and therefore alien to the majority Afro-Caribbean culture. It requires considerable psychological energy to both recognise difference and repress that recognition at the same time. Misir (2006) describes it as a cultural mosaic, while Patrick Taylor (2013) comes closest to the choreography of the various tensions when he describes this cultural co-habitation as a dance of visibly different nations who share a physical space, a plural transformative space (Carpenter, 2017) would like to suggest that the appropriate metaphor for the Caribbean psycho-ethnic dance is a "limbo", (Emrit, www.bestoftrinidad.com), in which the cultural minority bends back as much as possible, arms outstretched to both balance and embrace their Caribbean status, and inch their way under the pole of acceptance as authentic. Each engagement requiring greater and greater skill and flexibility. I believe that it is this limbo dance, along with the economic benefits that have pushed so many in the past to re-migrate to North America, where they can again assume the cloak of ambiguity, while practicing their Jewish faith undisturbed. It is good to be different, but not too different.

"The postcolonial concerns with hegemony and cultural hybridity Canclin (1990) sometimes described as creolization', are shared by a number of cultural historians…" (Burke, in Bennett and Frow, 2008, p. 107). These concerns are also shared by Jewish communities outside of the Caribbean as we have seen, albeit for the fear of assimilation. The concerns of the *ethnicists* in this instance is for pollution and corruption of what they deem as distinctly Jewish. An understandable concern given the motivation of wanting to preserve some notions of ethnic purity, the very notions for which Jews and Black have been persecuted over time. I think it is a primordial human instinct for self-preservation, that allows us to imagine that skin colour and phenotype features could signal a different species from ourselves. Man's nature is to classify, to compartmentalise in order to make sense of the world around us. Previous research carried out in the region demonstrates the politics of racial ambiguity and how changeable our ethnic categories can be. In 2008, Professor Devonish and the author carried out a minor experiment with a young man who, by the definition being used here, was an Indio-African Creole. He was tall, 6'2", thin, olive complexion, curly black hair, which he wore long enough that it could be left curly and bushy, slicked back, or placed neatly in a ponytail. We presented the same young man in 3 different guises, with his hair and clothing slightly adjusted to conform to different stereotypes. The result was a re-classification of the same young man into different ethnicities. "In Canada he was classified as Ethiopian, Ethiopians living in Canada in turn classified him as Eritrean, and in Europe he is seen as Somali, Arab and Black. In his native Guyana he is deemed Black and in Jamaica as Indian. It is clear from this and other attempts at examining stereotype notions that the concept of race can be subjective and situational according to culture (Carpenter and Devonish, 2008). Gordon Lewis describes the privilege of being this kind of alien hybrid, especially as depicted in the literature of the region and about the region. "What emerges from the literature is a picture of an urban bourgeoisie of a mixed cultural character, its members merging with each other in social intercourse, frequently, it is true, for reasons of survival as economically privileged groups of long standing (Jamaican Jewry)…" (Lewis, 1968, p. 38). It does not escape Lewis's attention, writing in this early period after independence that, "The general historical experience of the Caribbean Negro peoples, all in all has not been unlike the European Jew. Both of them have been uprooted peoples at the perennial mercy of the forces of migration and accident" (Lewis, 1968, p. 66). It is this affinity and shared history of displacement and suffering that Fanon references when he says, "The Jew and I: Since I was not satisfied to be racialized, by a lucky turn of fate I was humanized. I joined the Jew, my brother in misery" (Fanon, p. 92). It can be no mystery then when the displaced Jew and the displaced Negro find each other, why they might naturally intermarry and hyphenate. In hyphenation they find a strength that cannot be experienced or expressed as singular identities. They both benefit from the mutual experience of being visible to each other as socially excluded. The psychological benefits that accrue to the offspring of such unions may be questionable, particularly in societies that see Whiteness as privilege. In the Caribbean, the benefits are evident in the lived experience. What is in it for the Jew one might ask? Kritzen's, "What Kind of Man are You?" answers some of these questions.

Chapter 3

THE CARIBBEAN EXPERIENCE

In the early 1980's I flew back and forth between London, Mexico City and Jamaica. I was a British - Jamaican living and studying in Mexico City. In Mexico I lived predominantly in Jewish areas where residents parked their cars from Friday sundown to Saturday and could be seen walking to and from shul – school (understood as synagogue) on Shabbat. My Jewish friends were descendants of Jews from a variety of European and Middle Eastern countries who had sought refuge in Latin America. I remember returning to Mexico via Jamaica on one occasion and sharing a newsletter from the Share Shalom community in Kingston, Jamaica with my very close friend, Isaak. He was fascinated to see photographs of young Jewish, Black boys making their bar mitzvah. Isaak said to me, "They're Jewish?" When I responded, "Yes", he retorted with, "But they're Black?" The idea of black Jews had never occurred to him, although he had travelled widely. A Turkish Jew himself, growing up in Mexico City, he had never conceived of a person, who, like himself, had been living a hyphenated life as a Jamaican-Black-Jew, although his family was Mexican-Turkish-Jews. This response on the part of my close friend, led me to question how much was known about Jews by Jews and what would make one Jew identify another as distinctly Jewish.

JEW BY RELIGION

Among those Caribbean nationals who identify as Jewish are those who do not meet the Halachic standard of having a Jewish mother but are accepted by the Caribbean Jewish communities as being of a Jewish father and therefore Jewish tribe. A number of these persons actually grew up attending Hebrew school and synagogue, going through the various religious rites and indeed seeing themselves as separate from their Christian friends in the holidays and festivals they celebrated, the food they ate and the languages they worshipped in. They have completed *bar and bat mitzvahs*, and to all concerned are identified as Jews. Others who consider themselves Jewish by religion have certainly converted. We see this practise in particular among women married to Jewish men, who want to raise their children in keeping with the faith and culture. For so many others whose great and grandparents may have converted to Christianity or married a Christian partner, and subsequently abstained from any Jewish practice, they now feel the call to come "home" as one Jew in Curacao put it. There is no doubt as to the influence of the presence of Sephardim in the region, as can easily be deduced by the Portuguese sir names that abound. A quick glance at any telephone directory listing for the islands mentioned will reveal a host of such names, from Abrahams, to Zaade and countless more. Ironically, the great majority of persons bearing those names such as Delgado, Delvante, da Costa and others, may have no real idea that these names date back to the arrival of the Portuguese Jews in the region. When a group of people can trace their heritage for hundreds of years, going back more than 5 generations in a single place, it is understandable if they identify with that current within their blood line that has been most persistent. Many Caribbean Jews can still identify Jewish great, great, grandparents. An example of this is clearly demonstrated by the former President of Santo Domingo, Francisco Henriquez y Carvajal who was known to say, "I am a son of a Jewish father and a converso mother. She is not to blame that her family was forced to convert, and for me she is Jewish" (Arbell, 2002, p. 320).

In my research for this book I wanted to move away from the purely historical account of the Jewish Caribbean toward what I call, putting flesh on the bones. I wanted not only to look at the antecedents of the Caribbean Jewish communities in existence today, but I also wanted to hear about their lived experiences of being Jewish. I decided to interview select members of the community, with different experiences, yet one common identity. The questions I asked were very simple. I wanted to know, "What makes you a Jew?" "How do you experience your Jewishness in your everyday life?" and "What do you see for the future of Judaism in your Caribbean island community?" This chapter gives us a brief glimpse into the stories of Abrahm Ben Emanuel, Seth, Miriam and Jude.

JEWISH MOTHER-JEWISH FATHER

My interview with Abrahm Ben Emanuel was the first of the four reported here. He is a Historian who has a passion for genealogy. He is widely consulted by many researchers interested in Caribbean Jewry. Abrahm is tall medium build, with blue eyes that twinkle with mischief. He is extremely knowledgeable about Judaism and the history of the Jewish people. His quick wit and sharp intelligence make for easy conversation as we dart from topic to topic. Abrahm Ben Emanuel shares here some of the salient aspects of the history of the arrival of the Jews in the islands as well as his personal family journey, and the experiences that shaped his current view of his Jewish identity.

ABRAHM BEN EMANUEL'S STORY

> *Knowledge doesn't come by the remembering of facts only, but by questioning the facts. What I am telling you about is my own questioning about what is Judaism. I didn't have any Rabbi Samuel come and sit with me and tell me what Judaism is. I had to question it for myself. Why am I still a Jew? What is the belief system? Is it good for me? Is it bad for me?*

> Who is a Jew? It's somebody who believes in one G_d, in monotheism, believes in the ethics of the 10 commandments, believes that the interpretation of the Bible by the Rabbis in the Talmud is the order of how life should be managed or practised and that's basically who a Jew is. There is a mistake in the world in the western world that Judaism is an ethnicity and that's nonsense. Judaism has nothing to do with ethnicity at all. I don't think there is any pure ethnic anything. Everybody has a has mixed set of ancestry, for example it has been identified that my male ancestry is Phoenician but what does that make me? But I also have a clear knowledge that I have ancestry from the Iberian Peninsula, and I certainly know that my grandmother came out of the Ukraine, possibly with some, who knows, Mongol blood, I don't know. The ethnic Jew is a non-sequitur.

Abrahm Ben Emanuel's early adulthood was marked by both passion and tragedy. He married by the age of 25, to the love of his life, had three children and then lost his wife to cancer. His passion and his pain combined in a very short period of his life. At the same time, his memories of that period are warm and happy, and certainly convey the love they shared.

> I don't think there was a better Jew, in the sense of one woman that converted, than my late wife Shoshana, and she converted Rabbinically, and she came out of a Catholic background and she practised it [Judaism] to the best of her ability.

I ask him to explain what he sees as the different types of Jews. Since he does not believe in the concept of race and does not accept that there is any pure ethnicity in the world, I am curious as to whether Jew by heritage is a category he recognises.

> Jew by Heritage has a reality to it because you grow up with a cultural background. I have three daughters, they grew up with their mother who practised Judaism for the better part of her short life. And I'm very proud of what my daughters have done with my grandchildren. My daughters have been brought up Jewish and all my grandchildren [overseas] have all bar/bat mitzvahed with a standard of practice of Hebrew that I never even experienced in this island. And that is partly more heritage and culture than

anything else. Now, lineage, I think some people get a feeling that they have ancestors who were Jewish, and I have seen some interesting experiences in my own genealogical research, people who have three four generations of being brought up Catholic and they marry and find out they're Jewish. What is it? Is it lineage? I don't think it is lineage, it's more of a cultural background. I am taking a very pragmatic, and personal view, I'm not quoting Rabbis. In that sense our relationship in this exercise is almost as if I am co-authoring in that view.

As we settle in to the interview Abrahm Ben Emanuel shares some of the history of the community and some of the lesser known facts about how Judaism has evolved in the neighbouring islands. He has been a rich resource for many who want to have a full understanding of the life of the Caribbean Jews and indeed has been consulted for a great number of the books that have already been written on the topic. He continues by outlining the differences between being born of a Jewish mother and having a tribal inheritance from a Jewish father.

The Orthodox also accept the fact that a person who is born to a Jewish mother, regardless of whether she is practicing Judaism or not is automatically recognised as being a Jew, and that is another story. Because on the one hand you have the three definitions of Jews, this is actually transferred through the male line. But in terms of the acceptance by the Orthodox it is through the mother, because your mother is your mother no matter what. Again, I go back to the idea that anybody can practice Judaism, [which] has nothing to do with even who your mother or your father was, anybody can become a Jew, anybody can practise Judaism. The male now, are divided into three casts, the direct descendants of Abrahm Ben Emanuel the high priest - the Cohenim and then there are the Levites who are descended from David and then there are the ordinary Israelites. It is a male cast determination, so if your father was a Cohen you are a Cohen but if your mother was the daughter of a Cohen you're not. I am a Cohen. It is a male cast determination, which is different from the idea that a person is a Jew, if the mother or grandmother, even if you are three or four or five generations removed, as long as the matrilineal line exists, you are a Jew. That is the Halachic law. So, now there are problems, let me be very blunt, if my daughters go to Israel, the question is, is your mother Jewish, and the answer is yes, converted Rabbinically, then there is the question, was the conversion done according to their practices. Then that becomes an issue. So, if we take this to the extreme, and we go to the many places in the world, where Jewish men settled, the women that became the mothers of their children, who were not Jews, at the time, but practised Judaism in the way my late wife practised it, how then do you prove this to be Halachic law 200 years later? So, it becomes a bit of a nonsense, so long after. In my view if the mother converted through a Rabbi, ordained in Progressive, Conservatism etc., you must accept the conversion, that means that the whole business can be brought into play.

We discuss the distinction to be found in the liturgy and practise in his local synagogue that is an amalgamation of Sephardic and Ashkenazi Jews. The same community has mistakenly been described as Reform in one or two more recent internet sources and I want to clarify their position on this.

The congregation I belong to is a liberal conservative synagogue. What do I mean by that? The liturgy and the way we practise it in English is Progressive, nothing to do with Reform, which came out of Germany. [our practise] is Sephardic. I go to synagogue in New York and the practice is the same, I come to this island and with the exception of the transliteration in English, the service is the same.

Accepting that the Sephardic practices differ from those of the Ashkenazi, I want to know how they are different. I also notice that the Sephardim I have interacted with, take great pride in the fact that they have been in the Caribbean for 500 uninterrupted years. They show a fierce pride in the lengths they have gone to in order to preserve their Jewish heritage through persecution and conversion, secrecy and return.

It is an interesting question [about the how the Sephardim are different] we discussed this in Orlando last week. Those from the Iberian Peninsula are Sephardim, then there are the Mizrahi - they are Eastern Jews, them there are the Ashkenazi-Eastern European Jews primarily. It is a loose identity, many of the Sephardi today are mixed. I consider myself

Sephardic, but my grandmother was from the Ukraine, which is Ashkenazi. There is no such thing as pure Sephardim anymore, most Sephardics are mixed. The concept of a true Sephardic is trying to establish race again. My grandmother's family, Mordecai and Marshalleck, they came from Czechoslovakia. Depends on whether you call Czechoslovakia middle European or Ashkenazi. And funnily enough when I go to conferences I'm considered to be one of the outstanding Sephardim. The liturgies are totally different, the essence of Jewish practise is to read the Torah every week, and so the Parashas are the same. What is also interesting is that the main Sephardic synagogue in New York, but for instance, and I was there five weeks ago, the majority of the congregation are Ashkenazim and yet they practice the Sephardic liturgy. The primary Sephardic congregation in the Caribbean is Curacao. They practise in two synagogues, *Mikve Israel - Hope of Israel,* and then they have an Ashkenazi synagogue. Barbados, I don't know what their Sephardic practise is because their's disappeared. St. Thomas in the Virgin Islands I don't know what they practise is because they service lots of snow birds. Suriname is another one. The different language groups across the Caribbean have not made a significant difference in the practise, because Hebrew is Hebrew is Hebrew. The majority of the population that came were Dutch and Sephardic and many were Conversos who returned to the practise of Judaism.

We return to the conversation of Abrahm Ben Emanuel's own Jewish upbringing. He continues from his arrival as a young man in England. There he would visit with an Orthodox couple who he became very close to and who exposed him to life within their community and home. They were an Eastern European couple who had escaped the war and met in England.

My own history is that I was in London as a young man and visited with a Polish family, the woman had escaped the Holocaust and fled to Jamaica where she had been housed at the Gibralta Camp, Mona. She later went to the U.K. where she met her husband, who had managed to escape through Ireland and settle in England, where they met and married. I attended an Orthodox synagogue with them, and people would say, who is the Goy, with Miriam? Because I was blonde with blue eyes and Ashkenazi Jews are not blue eyed and blonde. They come out of Lithuania and Poland in the 17th century. It's one of the things which now, the DNA programme that I am now peripherally connected with. I have the [DNA] kits, I've given out some and they have mine already, so I know I'm Portuguese. They have mine now for 10 years now. I know my history. I did farm work for a year. I did manual labour for a whole year overseas.

He returns to his memories of his earlier years at home in the islands, with his step father and his mother. What it meant to be part of one of the most prominent Jewish families in the country, and what he learned from that experience.

I think my step father was seminal in my Jewish thinking. He told us things that he practised with his father, as the eldest son of a Syrian immigrant, and that he had also experienced in Israel with his aunt, his father's sister, who had come out of Damascus. And so, you questioned some of these things, so the concept of questioning was really the difference. And I didn't understand it until much more recently. You don't learn by rote. Knowledge doesn't come by the remembering of the facts only, but by questioning the facts. What I am telling you about is my own questioning about what is Judaism. I didn't have any Rabbi Samuel come and sit with me and tell me what Judaism is. I had to question it for myself. Why am I still a Jew? What is the belief system? Is it good for me? Is it bad for me?

Abrahm Ben Emanuel's questioning of his Jewish genealogy versus his identity is an existential dilemma that many who cross the line between what they know to be their heritage, and what they now seek to pursue outside of that heritage, might face. The question of whether being committed to a Jewish identity not only as heritage, but as spiritual practise and culture, flies in the face of living in an integrated union and raising children who in part, share a heritage that is different from yours, can be a defining one. The resolution of that existential question, "Who am I?" "How do I see myself and how do my beliefs and actions reflect my personal integrity?" is something that critical thinkers invariably have to face at some point in their life. Though the situations or circumstances that bring us to this point vary, the question remains the same. Erikson (1980) would say that we face this question at each defining stage of our: identity formation in adolescence; identity consolidation in adulthood (when our many roles are challenged); and identity integration, when we look back at the life cycle and assess if we have lived a life of integrity. For Abrahm Ben Emanuel, this is the final stage of his identity process as he grapples with his 8th stage in the life cycle - *integrity vs disgust or desp*air.

What happened to the community is a number of things. We have had some remarkable Rabbis, people who became highly recognised around the world and a number of Rabbinical leadership changes. By the end of the 19th century they had lost these Rabbinical exposures. Certainly, when my mother was growing up, and I'm going into the early 20s, she didn't have it, the Jewish education. Her grandfather read his prayers on a Friday and her aunt was the first woman to have a driver's license on the island. You had to come into the capital by buggy. Fast forward now to 1946, Rabbi Samuel came, and he was an English liberal, and that is very different from American Reform, and practised the Conservative Liberalism. But he didn't have the kind of Jewish education that I would like to impart to others today.

They didn't go out on a Friday night, but they didn't know why they didn't go out on a Friday night, the meaning behind these things. So, Rabbi Samuel leaves and Rabbi Harkema turns up and he was a more aggressive, dynamic individual. Now he did a lot for Judaism per se but not for the Jews. He popularised Judaism. He did something which I think was important, he did think, he encouraged thinking, and he encouraged what was in this island's sense, *tikun olam – heal the world,* with that idea the school was founded. And because Rabbi Harkema encouraged a number of things I became very, very exposed to a number of things. The last time I was in Israel 5 years ago I had lunch with the first Israeli Ambassador in 1972, I've know every Ambassador since. Our first Ambassador was Gideon Saguy. What can I tell you, I've been connected [He chuckles to himself].

JEWISH FATHER-GENTILE MOTHER

Intermarriage has been the consistent trend for those of the community who have decided to stay behind in the islands. Unlike other minority groups such as the Indians, Chinese and some Arabs, the custom of bringing a Jewish bride or husband from abroad, has not been a popular practice. In many instances the mothers have converted, and the children of intermarriage have been brought up in the customs and practice of Judaism (Arbell, 2000). The children usually have a bar/bat *mitzvah* even if they do not continue to attend *shul,* after leaving high school. Various sources on the history of the Caribbean Jews have noted the custom of migration to the United States, to join with other communities of Jews, to avoid intermarriage and assimilation, once the individual reaches adulthood. However, this is not strictly speaking the only motive for the migration patterns observed in the Caribbean and elsewhere in former colonies. There has been an active practice for centuries of college-aged children leaving for their education abroad. This practice is expected and is widespread among the middle classes, Jewish or otherwise. They will in fact, connect with their friends from home, on college campuses overseas and continue their lives fairly uninterrupted, returning for major holidays like Christmas, Easter and Summer. Whether they settle overseas permanently, has always been an option for these children, indeed their parents and grandparents have often set the standard for an overseas education. Those who return contribute to the development of local industries though the education and experience they acquire. In fact, the truth is that many overseas universities actively recruit Caribbean students for their Pre-university and University programmes.

Among those who grew up in a half Jewish home was Seth. He, his brother and sister were brought up in the Jewish community and went through all the rites of passage of the faith. They are fully immersed in the life and service of the community where they perform a number of roles. His story is similar to that of island children who are seen by the majority local community as white and therefore separate from them. Given his Jewish identity, attending a non-Jewish school made him further identify as a Jew, he was unique in the school he attended. Seth has warm brown eyes and an easy smile, which make him very approachable. His willingness to reach out to others and service as a marriage officer and spiritual leader means that he is often called on by members of the community for a variety of reasons.

SETH'S STORY

> What do I think of Jews? Industrious, priority placed on education, inventive, progressive, because that is how the families, certainly in Jamaica developed, very, very, humbly and by educating each other.

His father was a Jew and his mother a gentile. He grew up in extended family where all his immediate family, cousins and uncles practiced the Jewish faith. He grew up attending his local synagogue and undergoing all the appropriate rites. He has remained in his local community, serving as a religious leader of the synagogue. He has himself married a gentile, yet his children have been brought up in the faith and followed all the rites. "What makes me a Jew…it has nothing to do with birth, it has nothing to do with ethnicity, what makes me a Jew is that my understanding of *Adonai – G_d*, is what makes me a Jew. I was born of a Jewish father, and brought up a Jew, but none of that is what makes me a Jew". "Every Jew believes in one unseen G-d, [a Jew is] a person who believes and accepts the Torah as his book of religious study, a person who treats his neighbour as he would treat himself. Those to me are the fundamentals of Judaism. You could be any colour, you could be anyone, but these are the three fundamentals".

Seth remembers his days in school as a young boy, how he was different from his friends, how he was the only Jew in his class. He stayed home on the Jewish holidays. This separation he says, "…created in me a uniqueness, a difference, it didn't make me afraid like others, it made me stronger". The school he attended was Christian, however he continued to be an observant Jew throughout his schooling. In high school, it meant that he could not participate in the usual pastimes that Christian teenagers enjoyed, such as Saturday Matinees and other outings during Shabbat. This never bothered him, but rather cemented for him his Jewish identity. "Being a Jew created in me a mind-set that gave me the strength to say I am different, I am Jewish. Therefore, living that way, from those early days I was not allowed to go to school on the holy days. I didn't feel left out, I felt unique." The multi-ethnic composition of his high school allowed him more freedom of expression than his preparatory school experience. "The more I was able to identify [as Jewish], it made me respected among my peers. I wasn't ridiculed by my peers, I was respected".

At home they didn't keep kosher because his mother was not Jewish, and his father was not very observant, but through his own efforts in attending *shul* and Sabbath School he grew in the faith. He learned to observe the dietary laws for the festivals and holidays and others in the community he says, observe 90% of those laws too. So, there is a ceremonial observance. "We know our lineage is Portuguese, we know we were here from the 1500s, before the English, because the historical records show that the family helped the English to fight the Spanish and gave them information against them. There are members of this family in North America, central America and Latin America. Because we were traders, because we had the trader background."

I asked Seth what comes to his mind when he thinks of the stereotypical Jew? Did he think of some of the more negative labels such as, mean, tricky, money-loving, etc., he said no, these were more labels applied to a North American stereotype and not in the Caribbean according to his experience. His own idea of the Jewish-Caribbean stereotype is.

Industrious, priority placed on education, inventive, progressive, because that is how the families, certainly in this island developed, very, very, humbly and by educating each other. They began their trade on a bicycle and even the ones who built buildings and won competitions and started newspapers with very little and built it up over time. The stereotypes of the stingy, mean Jew, when I hear that I think of the European Jew, certainly not the Caribbean stereotype.

He believes that the wealth that Jews were able to enjoy, coming from very humble backgrounds, was due to the religious base they had. And that the very prosperity they managed to gain, came back on them in the form of envy and jealousy from others in the society. He remembers his own father as a financially well-off man who worked his way up in the family business. But he also remembers his dad as a man of moderate tastes who spent his wealth on educating his children, having the occasional family vacation and being a devoted family man. "He could have built a very big house and a fancy car, but he was a family man who continued to live in a town house with a modest car so that we could travel from time to time. And he sacrificed his own comfort for us, his children so that we could have a good education."

Seth says the reputation of Jews as frugal, is not grounded in reality because, "there is nothing a Jew could do to impress anybody, because it is going to come back on you". He points to a lesson he has learned recently as a 57-year-old man. He knew a wealthy Jewish family who he feels lived more than modestly. They afforded themselves very little in life. Yet when the last member of the family living in the island died they left behind a legacy of an international-standard race track for the school the family used to attend. All their remaining wealth went to educating others. He describes this as typically Jewish, the fact that they had a purpose all along in scrimping and saving. He goes on to say,

> *Tikun olam - heal the world,* in my life is my service to my community to make others aware of the positives of G_d's life. That's one aspect of it. My actions, not by my words only do I live. I help charities, I teach, I help others to learn and that's how I have lived my whole life. In the ways that I conduct my affairs, in the modest way I live with no interest in abject luxury, nor in abject poverty, I see no purpose in that.

He doesn't describe himself as a pious man, a holy man or even a man who has achieved great education, but he feels his life is directed by the philosophy and spirituality of being a Jew. He believes in living a life of charity, of giving of his time and money and skills in the service of others.

> My idea of charity may not be as holy or high or spiritual, but I certainly give. I also believe that charity is not something that can be measured by the amount. A lot of people believe that charity is money. I don't think so, in many areas I give of myself, my time, living my life in ways that add to the whole concept of *Tikun olam - heal the world"*.

He believes in living a moderate life of purpose, and in being a fair example to others. In his family all the boys have his father's first name and then their own second name. In this way they honour their father and his memory and legacy is still alive. Seth leads the service in his local synagogue and has been doing so for over 20 years. He counts on the teachings of Rabbis who inspire him to help the congregation see how the scriptures are teaching you a life lesson every time.

> If G_d is the primary, and understanding what G_d wants of you, is it something that needs to be shown (as in the loud singing etc.,) or something that needs to be explained?

He believes Judaism is more interested in explaining what G_d's purpose is for us in everyday life. His views on the future of Judaism in the island is expressed in the following statements.

> I think the future of Judaism in this island has to focus on bringing or attracting returnees. Judaism [here] has never been a group that proselytizes, it's never been a large group, it's always been a smaller group of more intense worshipers. I think some will tell you it will survive, it will survive with smaller and smaller remnants. There are significant numbers of people in this island who follow practices of Judaism. There are groups that have formed up in some pockets of this island and I don't mean Jews for Jesus, they are very interested in Jewish practice. They haven't got to the point where they have a service, but all the Torah study are like ours. They use the *Shema - prayer* etc., There are different viewpoints…we have to look at it in more practical ways. Going through a conversion is a relative situation. Most of the people who come and worship with us have no delusions of going to Israel and live, they would rather go to America. Judaism started out as paternal, through time it changed due to war and

pillage. We tend sometimes to allow our social and cultural to dictate. The word we like to use for our worship here is Progressive.

When I interviewed Seth, I was reminded of a small book, Half Jew" by D. M. Miller about being half Jewish. And although Seth does not see himself as "half", his "*identification*" by the Orthodoxy would certainly not qualify as Jewish, given his mother was not a Jewess. Miller raises an important question, which no doubt has been on the minds of many such Jews, "When does your father count?" It is a serious issue for many Jews who come from these hyphenated families. Miller describes this denial of his father's role in his ethnic identity, "It matters when you are ethnically Jewish on your father's side, but people want to erase your father's ethnicity completely from your heritage…Your father's side is merely a void, a vacuum", (Miller, D. M. 2017, p. 28). Growing up in a Caribbean Jewish community Seth was spared that identity crisis, in fact his Jewishness has been a source of great pride and purpose.

JEWISH BY CONVERSION

Someone who identifies as a Jew and takes some kind of steps to mark themselves as a Jew. Everything that it means to be a Jew, then that's my identity.

Miriam had been living among Jews on three continents for most of her adult life. She has lived in London, New York and the Caribbean among Jews. In the UK she lived in conservative Jewish areas and in the U.S. among Hasidic Jews. She has studied, worked and lived in these communities and is therefore well acquainted with the lifestyle. Miriam is an example of so many converts to Judaism. She has a deep respect for the faith, culture and practices and is an observant Jew. She has no lineage. She traces her long journey from the Christian church where she was a minster. Having grown tired of Sunday worship she began keeping Sabbath simply because it was more comfortable for her. She then began to read about keeping Sabbath and what that meant. This initial step, led to greater interest in the history of Christianity and from the Anglican church she moved to the Charismatic movement to Messianic Judaism and now considers herself between Conservative and Orthodox in her belief and worship.

MIRIAM'S STORY

> *Being Jewish first of all has to do with identity. Identifying historically and culturally...with [the people] Israel in the land and in diaspora. Identifying means it's not just nominal, whether you are a secular Jew or whether you return to what you originally knew to be your Jewish identity, or whether you convert as I did. It means taking on whatever challenges and antisemitism and the persecution, taking everything on, taking on the cultures.*

Her process was a gradual one and she has been attending the same local synagogue where she was welcome, for 17 years. She converted 12 years ago. As a child she lived in England and attended private schools where the children and principals were primarily Jewish. Her best friend was also Jewish and wanted to make her a Brownie in her Jewish pack. She describes her parents as secular and that the promptings and initiatives were her own. She attended Christian churches on her own and with her neighbours. What struck her as inauthentic was the fact that Christianity was a branch of the tree, and not the Abrahamic tree itself. For her, the cognitive dissonance occurred between what she was being taught in church and what the facts of Bible history demonstrated. She self describes as Conservadox.

> *I believe in an actual Messiah not just a messianic age. I do believe in resurrection and multiple dimensions. When I'm in the States I will visit with a Spanish Conservative synagogue. I've been to Chabad services, Moroccan, I also had an Orthodox friend who took me to her Orthodox synagogue. What I liked about the Spanish-Portuguese synagogue is that they have a women's Torah service and they have a talk.*

Miriam expressed the view that she did not see herself as ever being drawn to the teachings of the Reform group, yet some of her views were more liberal than I would imagine from someone who identifies in part with the Orthodox community and even at times, Conservative Jews. I asked her to explain for me why she felt that Reform Judaism was not an option.

> Why Not reform? They change some of the prayers like the *Amidah – Standing Prayer*, which I don't like. It's funny because British Reform is more like Conservative. Some of the things don't fit for me. I guess I'm a bit more observant than Reform might be. I think Torah needs to be interpreted in a contemporary way, but at the same time, I think Reform might go a bit too far. Like in the States, when I was living in Riverdale I guess I could have attended an Orthodox temple, but I didn't know how I would be received. I used to live in an Orthodox community in England, and in Kew Gardens there was a store that said "Organic" so I went in there and they were so suspicious, and I didn't feel comfortable, because I looked different from them. And that was my first experience, and later on when I lived there I felt it wasn't so bad.
>
> I was reluctant to attend Orthodox services. I lived in Orthodox areas and I felt that when you went into the stores people looked at you suspiciously, but the people in the neighbourhood were very nice. The lived experience of being Jewish. It is a heart connection, this is for life. I keep Sabbath. The Jewish character [is] to demonstrate love, lift up those who are down, that sense of responsibility for others.
>
> It means that I am a Jew because I believe in the G_d of Abraham Isaack and Jacob, and because I am part of a people that have a covenant to live in a certain way to recognise G_d, to demonstrate G_d's love to other people. G_d is life itself and he is the source of our existence and his life and his love looks after us and helps each person to be the best they can be. Justice, mercy and compassion. We have a responsibility for those who are weaker.

During her travels around the world, Miriam experienced a number of Jewish lifestyles, liturgy and culture. She herself speaks of the Jewish cultures, recognising that there are a variety of ways that people express their identity. In her early adulthood she experienced a pull towards the Jewish experience, the suffering of the Jews and the will to survive and thrive that they demonstrated in their history. Miriam found she could not explain this pull and connection she felt with Judaism and the Jewish people. In our interviews he describes the first instance that she became fully conscious of this connection.

> Part of this connection is also inexplicable for me. Even before I thought about conversion I wanted to visit the museum of Jewish Heritage in New York, and my husband said "No", I almost didn't but when I got there, and I saw the exhibits I felt like an adopted child who had found their way home. I was crying, and I didn't understand why. I felt his deep literal connection. One of my Orthodox friends said you were at Sinai, you are Jewish. I don't know how to explain that, but she said you are Jewish. She observes all the holidays and observes the dietary laws but doesn't keep kosher. I discovered that even some Kenyans and Ghanians don't mix meat and dairy, so there must be something to it, it's not just Jews who observe it. I think for me I see things on multiple dimensions, so even the Bible I look at it from different angles. So even the health, when you practice the dietary laws you find you have less illness.

After years of study and attendance at *shul*, she made her *bat mitzvah* and has been serving in her local congregation since.

RUEBEN'S STORY

> My Judaism for me is essential as breathing. I do not need to wear my yarmulke – religious men's Jewish skullcap, but I don't necessarily need to put on black and white. It is how I live my Jewish identity, how I treat people, it is how I train my children, how I observe Shabbat. How I eat It is what I eat, when I eat.

He also converted as an adult and has no lineage. He is an observant Jew who is bringing up his children in the faith. He was baptised a Catholic at birth, but later attended a number of schools and Christian churches, none of which held any appeal for him. His household was liberal in their religious beliefs and he was therefore allowed to make a conscious choice as to which faith he would call his own. Interestingly, like Miriam, who also converted, Rueben had a pivotal moment when he felt the call of Judaism. He too encountered discrepancies between the Bible and the practise of Christianity, which led him to look for new answers to his spiritual questions.

> They [my children] will not be seen as Jewish, but they will know what Jewish life is about and they can convert when the time comes to do their *bar mitzvah*. What defines me as a Jew is I got sick and tired of following, following behind sort of everybody else to say what defines your religion. I did not want to be handed something. Typically, everybody in the island is a Christian. But if you ask them what is Christianity what do you know about Christianity? Particularly for a person of colour, black person. They tell you they have Praise & Worship, but do they know what it is? Do you even know the dogma or anything? I grew up pretty much…was supposed to be Catholic at the time. And my mother was more Evangelical than anything else. When they were going to do confirmation, my mother was the one who said, never accept anything until you understand it. Make a conscious decision. I tried a number of things at first. I tried Catholicism because I was supposed to be one. The teachings didn't line up, so I thought naah. Then I went to a private Seventh Day Adventist Church and that was mostly Old Testament, so I was influenced by that, but then if they say that their teachings are based on the Old Testament, but you are doing a different thing. If you look at Christianity today, you realise that much of it has nothing to do with the teachings in the Bible. Most Christians worship on Sunday, but if you ask them why they don't know. Too much of Christianity has its taint in blood.

While he admits that the enquiring and intellectual nature of Judaism and Jewish thought appeals to him, he also affirms that this is not his primary reason for converting. He is clear about his connection to the spirituality, liturgy and lifestyle of Judaism.

> A lot of people also [see the] appeal of Judaism because it allows you to hold a conversation without talking rubbish. But it's not only the

intellectuality of it. There is a fundamental spiritual side to Judaism that a lot of people don't explore. A lot of people will say I am not drawn to Judaism because you go every week and say the same prayers, and I say do you pay attention to the prayers that you say? Do you even understand what you are reading? It's not enough to go with your *Sidur – Prayer Book,* and read. If you are only reading you are just regurgitating. You need a certain level of programming to allow you to understand the basics. When a child goes to temple, like my children when they start off at an early age and they learn the Shema and they learn all of these prayers. If you are a good Jewish parent you should be explaining to your child, in a gradual way until the stage of their *bar mitzvah*, what is your responsibility to the community, what is your responsibility to yourself and what is your responsibility to G_d. It's not just to have a big bar mitzvah party and you do your *haftorah – reading from the prophets*, portion and you're done, that's it. I think too many people they stop at the *bar mitzvah* stage. I read in the book by Delvante that the islands had so many synagogues that Jews were coming here to learn Judaism, and so many famous Rabbis were here. And my how times have changed, not to throw away 500 years of tradition. This is the pull towards Chabad, because they see this guy with his black coat and his *tzit tzit* – ritual fringes and tassels, and whatever hat, they say, hey that is a Jew. But what people don't know is that in Poland, you walk around in your knicker bockers and high stockings, your black coat and hat and this was a way to make you stand out, it was a badge of shame. You single them out for persecution.

When asked to explain, what makes him a Jew in his everyday life. He expresses how natural it is for him to practise his faith and to live the Jewish lifestyle. He describes it as breathing. He is fully immersed in his Judaism but believes that moderation in all things is key.

My Judaism for me is essential as breathing. I do not need to wear my *yarmulke* but I don't necessarily need to put on black and white. It is how I live my Jewish identity, how I treat people, it is how I train my children, how I observe Shabbat. How I eat It is what I eat, when I eat. I was with a couple of Muslim friends and we went for dinner to have fish and they were having shrimps or something of the sort, we went to a seafood restaurant, and I look at the menu and I said to them the only thing I can eat on this menu is the fish fillet, and they said, "Oh you guys don't eat shellfish", and I say "No we don't". I'm not going to run down the restaurant because they [eat different]. If you want to order your Hawaiian pizza with your ham on it, then go ahead. I define for myself how to be an observant Jew, and I say to myself this is what I believe. And inside my house we don't have it in there. I don't understand how anyone in their right mind would eat meat and dairy, because the only thing that dairy does is it slows down your system and then you have meat sitting in your stomach and you add dairy to it. You going to have health problems. I tend to shy away from anything that seems too far on a sect or goes to the extreme, I believe in moderation. I don't push my beliefs on anybody else. For me, my Jewish identity has evolved to the point where when I pray it's just talking to God. When I look at a menu, I don't have to think about what to eat, I just don't eat certain things.

Presently, Rueben is living and working in Africa with his family. Their jobs involve travelling and this gives him the opportunity of 'charging' his spiritual batteries as he puts it, by visiting with the Jewish communities around the world.

The thing is living here in Africa, there is no synagogue, there is no active community, there is no major fellowship. I say my *Amidah – Standing Prayer,* and my prayer on Shabbat morning. I get up and read my *tehillim - Psalms.* It's like having a cell phone and when I go home [to the islands] I charge it. When I'm here I'm like a cell phone that's unplugged. One of the things I remember, is the first time I went to our local synagogue back home, It was *Rosh Hashana – Jewish New Year,* I was standing in the doorstep like a kid who was looking through the window of a candy store, saying "Can I come in, can I come in?" and one of the members signalled to me to come in. It was so long ago I was a young man with a full head of hair, no grey hairs and 100lbs lighter, so that was over 20 years ago.

Rueben has had so many spiritually enriching experiences as a Jew throughout his travels worldwide, that it reinforces his faith as an observant Jew. Of these the *brit milah – circumcision ceremony,* of his two youngest boys, born in Germany, was a signal moment for the entire family.

Some of the things that have affirmed for me my Jewishness as I have travelled around the world is the experience of the welcoming of people. I remember the children getting their *brit milah* in Germany, and the desperate struggle of finding a *mohel – circumsiser,* for that issue. How I found the *mohel*, there is one single Sepharidi synagogue in Berlin and I asked my wife to get in touch with them, and they wouldn't perform it, but they gave her the telephone number for this Dr. Matalon in Munich. My son didn't stick to the plan, he came two weeks early and when my wife called up this Dr. Matalon she just said we don't do that and hung up the phone, just like that she dismissed my wife. And there I was, sitting in the kitchen and my whole world shattered, thinking this kid has to get a brit. I got back on the internet and found another Sephardic Rabbi, because our people tend to be more welcoming, and I left a message on his voice mail. Ten minutes later Rabbi Nacama called back and gave me some other names. We went to a *mohel* and she organised a minyan and she prepared the certificate for the sake of if he wants to convert. Later I called her and said, listen we have another one and she spoke to my wife if she was ready to convert, and she said not fully yet. But that *mohel* had health issues with her husband. I called back Rabbi Macnama and they gave me another number, and we found a Rabbi Ruben from Azerbaijan. I didn't know there were Sephardim in Azerbaijan, and he asked if my wife was converting, and I said she is in the process and he said that's good enough for me, and he said come. And so, he got a minyan and they invited us for Shabbat, I think Purim was coming up or something, but that's the difference. And my wife said my gosh, [she] never stopped talking about how holy the experience felt, just a handful of people in the synagogue. It was like you stepped in the presence of somewhere that you felt that the purpose was prayerful, and people were praying, and it was so spiritual.

He places a great deal of value on the larger community of Jews and the common spiritual bond that is shared among Sephardim. He sees that as a 'common language'. He is observant of the dietary laws but is not slavish in his observance of the festivals and holy days. Rueben is also cautious of where he goes for worship and which communities he becomes involved with. He is as concerned with not causing offense as with being offended by other Jews who do not accept and recognise his Jewish identity.

Once you have that common language, that common bond and purpose it is easy to be drawn to each other. That's not true for all streams of Judaism. I find this is more true of Spharic Jews, we tend to gravitate to each other like moths to flame. But Judaism also has for me what I call my pet peeves is that we tend to run around on the holidays and make a big deal out of it. Personally, speaking the only holidays that really matter to me are Passover and Shuvot, Yom Kipur and *Rosh Hashana* for obvious reasons.

We definitely keep a kosher home and we only eat *brit milah* meat because now we live in Africa and there is a butcher nearby. Even when I fly we only eat *kosher – proper*, meals, plus it always come first, I don't know why.

In our family there is this open secret that we are really Rodrigues, but it doesn't really matter to me now because I think it's important for me to set a standard for my children that they can identify with. This summer we are going to Berlin and the children are going to be enrolled in a Jewish school and they won't be recognised as Jews and they tell me we can become members in the synagogue and the children can *bar mitvah* if you stay in Berlin. Don't tell me that if you don't recognise them, because we are a family. But I've said I will go to the Sephardic synagogue, I will attend there.

For Rueben, the future of Judaism in the islands will ultimately depend on our willingness to adapt and to begin to reach out to others, inviting them to understand what Judaism has to offer. This is a practise that is strongly avoided among our communities. It is only with the introduction of the Chabad movement that any proselytizing has taken place. An important issue that he raises is the fact that all worshippers in Judaism share a common language, Hebrew. This was also raised by Abrahm, and the fact that the common language and liturgy unites Jews everywhere. The small differences in the way the services are conducted have not broken that unity and common language bond. This is significant in that no matter where you attend service around the world, it will likely be in Hebrew. Rueben never stops speaking about the hospitality and generosity he has been shown by the Jewish community internationally. You get. strong sense of how important it is to Rueben that his Jewish identity be expressed in community.

We have to get over our reluctance to proselytize. The people who are in the community need [to]. We don't walk around with banners pretending to be holier than though. The larger community of island dwellers want to know that there are other options. I don't think we are paranoid of others finding out who we are, our doors are always open.

In a Conservative synagogue in Berlin, a very nice man named Walter, invited me to stay in his home. He said, "Rueben, 'The next time you're in Bavaria, my doors are open, please come and stay with me." One old lady asked me, 'Whose child are you again,' this was in the Balkans, I think she was Greek. When people who are of Arab descent look at me they think I am Moroccan. In a little Moroccan synagogue in Israel, in Elat I was standing at the door weighing up my options and a man called to me, he said come in. And I made up the minyan and it was quite an experience.

JEWISH BY CULTURE

[Judaism] has no dogma and lacks entirely any formal catechism which all believing Jews would accept.... One must abandon absolutes in ritual and in dogma and examine instead the broad philosophy which underlies our faith. What we believe about the Bible, about miracles, about life after death, is secondary to what we believe about human potentialities and our responsibilities toward our fellow men. (Herzig, 2012, p. 4-5).

Despite the fact that Judaism does not have any dogma, its religious practices are indeed rooted in culture and as other lifestyle religions it is pretty impossible to separate the festivals, celebrations, foods and observances from everyday life. Even Jews who no longer attend *shul*, after their *bar/bat mitzvah*, continue to participate occasionally in festivals and holy days. It is virtually impossible for the average urban dweller to avoid the many Jewish food items and vocabulary that have become commonplace in the average person's life. *Jewish Culture and Customs* (Herzig, 2012), contains a mini glossary of words that are easily recognisable by most urban dwellers from, *bagel* to *zayde (grandfather)*. The evidence of Jewish cultural products, arts and language interwoven into the fabric of secular, everyday life, is in part a gateway to the spiritual life that many Jews have left behind.

Their view that Judaism cannot separate culture from religion as the practices of its people are rooted in religious belief seems to be contradicted by the more than 40% of Jews in Israel and a similar percentage in the U. S., who declare themselves as secular (Pew Research Centre, 2016). Gary Tobin, former Head of the Institute for Jewish and Community Research, has been involved in studies of Jewish culture in the U. S. He concluded that, "The dichotomy between religion and culture doesn't really exist. Every religious attribute is filled with culture; every cultural act filled with religiosity (Tobin, 2002, https://www.myjewishlearning.com/article/jewish-cultural-identity/). It seems that the trend in Jewish behaviour has been moving away from religion and towards spirituality. What on the face of it, appears to be a contradiction between secular Judaism and religious practise, is the desire of many non-practising Jews to take part in the cultural life of the communities they live in. Rabbi Eric H. Yoffie, President Emeritus Union of Reform Judaism explains that,

> No matter how much they may scoff at religious belief [Cultural Jews], if you ask them "WHY do you identify with the Jewish people?" they will inevitably refer to values such as social justice, hospitality and *mentschlikeit* (decency). — values that are grounded in the sacred texts of Jewish religious tradition and that have endured solely because of the authority that the religious tradition imposes. (Yoffie, 2013)

In the Caribbean we have already noted the full synagogues on the Holy Days and yet during the rest of the year the average attendance is less than 50 persons at any given service. The numbers of Jews who count as members of the communities is invariably several times more than those who attend. The good news may well be that the secular aspects of Judaism, which have ensured the infiltration of Jewish customs and culture into the everyday fabric of Caribbean life will lead to better engagement with the next generation. That is certainly what Roger Bennett of Charles Bronfman Philanthropies hopes for. "We have a lot to learn about the use of culture as a means to an end, especially in terms of engaging the next generation of

Jews. (My Jewish Learning, https://www.myjewishlearning.com/article/jewish-cultural-identity/). We examine the role of cultural similarities and differences in forging new pseudo-Jewish identities' the infusion of pop culture with Jewish biblical influences; and the ways in which the tradition of outreach among the Chabad movement is influencing Judaism in the Caribbean, in Chapter 4.

Chapter 4

MODERN ADAPTATIONS

While working as a University lecturer in Britain, I had the pleasure of teaching a wide range of graduate students from no less than 20 countries each week. They were in the UK to finish PhD degrees, many of them were already respected professionals in their home countries. One day I was approached by a female student who recounted a story of encountering a Black Jew on the train in London. She was puzzled. This woman she had encountered introduced herself and told the student that she was a Black Jew, an original Jew. Her hair was matted into thin locks that spread down her back and she was dressed in the red, green and gold colours of her tribe. I explained with a smile, that the woman was Rastafari. This of course led to more explanations about what exactly is Rastafari and how they come to be Black Jews.

I have included in this Chapter, two alternative ways of viewing what it means to be a Jew, and because they appear to be at opposite ends of a religious continuum of Jewishness. The first, Rastafari originates in Jamaica but has now spread out from that tiny island to the rest of the world and has been adapted and adopted by all ethnicities. The second, Chabad, originates in Mezibush in the Ukraine as a form of Chasdic Judaism and has spread throughout the Caribbean. Ironically both Israel and Jamaica are geographically almost the same size and both have had a tremendous and disproportionate influence on the rest of the world.

THE RASTAFARI

Some of its proponents having little understanding of the teachings, while others, eager to embrace Rastafari have gone to great lengths to understand the philosophy. To begin with, Rastafari is a religion that started in Jamaica, in the Caribbean and has a following of an estimated 700,000 to 1 million worldwide (BBC, 2009). There are several branches of Rastafari, referred to as "Mansions", these include Nyabinghi, Bobo Shanti and the Twelve Tribes of Israel. Members of the faith identify as the true Israelites or Black Jews. This belief is based on the association of the faith with the late emperor of Ethiopia, Haile Selassie – The Conquering Lion of the Tribe of Judah. Rastafari religious symbols include aspects of Ethiopian and Jewish symbolism. Selasie is a direct descendant of King David of the Solomonic line and the Ethiopian Queen of Sheba, through their son, Menyelek. Rastafari see Selasie as the Messiah Incarnate (Jah Rastafari). The teachings of the Rastafari faith are built on the earliest writings of 1st century, Ethiopian religious and literary tradition of the Kebra Negast, "Glory of the Kings" and select Old Testament or Torah portions. The purpose here is to shed some light on how, what may be seen as Judaic practices, symbols and scriptures are incorporated into the Rastafari movement and worship practices of these "Black Jews".

Rastafari as a group, enjoy a peculiar relationship with the modern Jew. In some instances, and especially among the unschooled members of the faith, there is a generally friendly and respectful relationship with Jews as well as other religious groups. On the other hand, the Rastafari indoctrinated by the teachings of Leonard Howell, a follower of Garvey in the 1930's and later Prince Emmanuel Charles Edwards, may have an ambivalent relationship with the Jew, who he sees as a White usurper. Howell replaced the White Supremacy paradigm with one of Black Supremacy, thereby providing third and fourth options for Rastafari belief in the building of his own paradigm. Their beliefs include the rejection of the current Jews as authentic and instead the assertion of the Rastafari as the only authentic Jews. It is no accident that the seeds of Rastafari were sown in the turbulent 1930s that Stuart Hall (2017) spoke about earlier. With growing unrest and a call for Black self-reliance that rang out from the U.S. to the Caribbean, there now was a greater focus on Africa and all things African. Specifically, the prophecies and teachings of Marcus Garvey (a Jamaican living in the United States), galvanised large groups of U.S. Blacks, forming them into a movement of cooperatives and predicting the rise of an African King. Garvey founded the Garveyite Movement in his adopted country, America and was a charismatic and forceful leader of the Black American community, mobilising cooperatives for employment and building of Black pride in the US and Caribbean. Through a series of articles in Plain Talk - The Garveyite paper, L. F. C. Mantle was, "instrumental in crystallizing the ideology of Ethiopianism" (Post 1970, 196). By identifying all blacks as Ethiopians and as Jews, by placing Ethiopia at the head of Egyptian civilization, and connecting modern Italy with Ancient Rome. A key concept that took hold for the Garveyites and soon to be Rastafari was that all Africans were Ethiopians and all Ethiopians Jews (Chevannes, 1994, p. 42). Notwithstanding the fact that this miss-representation of the 54 nations on the continent of Africa was geographically inaccurate, the masses who were looking for liberation and leadership found this belief deeply affirming. In 1930 Ras Tafari Makonen, was crowned Emperor Haile Selasie of Ethiopia and was soon to be in a conflict with Italy under Musolini, who had invaded his country causing him to flee to Britain for four years. Selassie was later to regain his throne, leading his army in battle himself, thereby proving that his titles were a fulfilment of Garvey's prophecies. For the Rastafari all eyes were on Ethiopia, and Rasta seeks to emulate the Emperor Haile Selasie - Conquering Lion of the Tribe of Judah, who they see as a G_d incarnate, and his Queen Princess Menen Asfaw. Emperor Selasie himself denies being a G_d-Man and has never worn the traditional Nazarene "dreadlocks" that identifies the Rastafari, and he was never an adherent of the faith, but rather a member of the Ethiopian Orthodox Church and a Christian throughout his life.

In speaking with current Rastafari we gain an understanding of a more modern take on the Jewish-Rastafari connection. The explanation of the ways in which Rasta now view themselves has to do with the example of Haile Selasie as the foundation stone, that positions everything else. In mainstream popular culture Rasta has taken on a pop image of dreadlocks hair styles and the use of the Ethiopian flag colours and a frivolous marijuana – smoking riske individual. Ethiopia is the metaphorical Africa, not the literal one, although there is a community of repatriated Afro – Caribbean Rastafari at Shashamane in Ethiopia. The 'mansions' of Rastafari, as in the various tribes and practices, is a starting point for understanding the connection to the tribes of Israel. The recognition of the 12 tribes of Israel (Rueben, Simeon, Levi, Judah, Dan, Naphtali, Gad Asher, Issachar, Zebullon, Joseph, Ephraim, Benjamin) as the foundation of the Jewish and world peoples, translates into a belief in the Black Jew as descended from Judah, in the living form of King Selasie.

Rasta is a modern appropriation of this tribal descent through its teachings and practices. The Kebra Negast, provides the genealogical authenticity for Selasie as the descendent of King David. Today there is no homogenous Rastafari, the leadership is plural and the peculiarities of each branch of the religion distinguishes it slightly from the others, but the *inity* – *unity*, of the faith remains. With its roots in the Ethiopian Orthodox church of Haile Selasie, Rasta balances its foundations in Christianity and the rejection of same, as it wouldn't want to be associated with the White Christ of movies and legend. It is in the *livity* – *lifestyle* that the contradictions of these two polarities are reconciled. While Rasta makes its spiritual journey from the Caribbean through the prism of Judeo Christian adaptations to the world its many morphisms have united some and fractured others in their search for a spiritual home in the ideological Israel.

RASTAFARI & JUDAISM

Rastafari belief is informed by select passages from the English translation of the Bible: "Song of Songs", "Lamentations chapter 4, verse 8," "Lamentations chapter 5 verse 10", "Joel 2:8 and Habukkah 2:10", "Job, chapter 30 verse 30" (Dvorin, 1998, 5). Dani Dvorin a Jew, in his research on Rastafari came away somewhat disappointed in the conclusions that the group derived from the English translations of Hebrew verses and in most cases, misinterpretations of the literary devices and Hebrew grammar, which denotes male and female gender. Regrettably, this is no different perhaps from the experience of discussing the scriptures from a Christian perspective where the tendency is to cherry - pick passages that support a particular view, while ignoring context and often the larger passage the scripture is taken from. If Dani Dvorin (1998) was disappointed with what he found in the discrepancies between the scriptural interpretations of the Torah and the Rastafari professed faith, then Evan Salzberg, another Jew (2009) had the opposite experience. Salzberg describes the Rastafari in more positive tones and focusses on the aspects that bear any similarity, such as the dietary laws, symbols, commandments and dress for women. These are more superficial items but bear mentioning in light of the Kosher requirements for Jews. Adherents of the Rastafari faith also have their own dialect "Dread Talk" (Pollard, 2000), where words that are used in English are taken at a literal face value and reversed to mean the opposite of the English form, other words are derivatives of the English. If the Rastafari can in their *"livity"* (daily life or lifestyle), maintain a diet that is essentially Kosher, then it is not too hard to see how Jews may also keep kosher in the island. The difference is that the Rastas *"ital"* diet is a vegetarian, salt-free one that includes fish with scales but avoids all forms of preserved foods in cans. The closer to its natural state a food is, the better it is thought to be for the body. A more recent visitor to the island has been Rabbi Smuleh Boteach, wrote a review for "The Jerusalem Post", of his visit with the Rastafari community in April, 2018. "Many Rastas wear the Jewish star of David with a lion in the middle around their necks. Their diet is essentially kosher, bereft as it is of any animal or dairy products...All over Jamaica one can find vegan restaurants to cater to Rastafarians" (Boteach, 2018). Rastafari also use the Jewish six-point star and *magen* shield of David, as well as the lion as identifying markers. These along with the colours of the Ethiopian flag – red, green and yellow are associated with the faith and many musical artists use these symbols on their album covers and paraphernalia. The 13 commandments of the faith are unlike the 10 commandments of the Mosaic law, and only the second is similar. In Rasta speak/Dreadtalk, Jah is the name for Jehovah or G_d.

2) One must know and acknowledge the Bible and the teachings of Jah Rastafari above all things". Almost all their commandments make reference to the person of Ras Tafari. The 13th commandment seeks repatriation [back to Africa], which while not a commandment of the Jewish faith, could be considered an aspiration of the law of *Aliyah* Jewish state, 13) Repatriation is a must for all Rastafarians. Repatriation from

Babylon (western concepts and false teachings) to Zion land, the Promised Land, African Land. A physical and spiritual repatriation to the land of 'I n I' (our) fore-parents, with clean hands and pureness of heart (Salzberg, 2009).

Women are encouraged to dress modestly, cover their heads, not show too much skin, not wear makeup or process their hair in any way. This is more in keeping with some of the Orthodox Jewish customs. Another aspect of Rasta life for women, which is often overlooked is the laws around menstruation. Similar to halachic laws of *niddah* (menstrual purity), Rasta women are required to separate themselves during the time of menstruation from chores such as food preparation. It is thought that their vibrations and the external forces they bring during this time can affect their men. Whether some communities continue to practice a form of ritual bath, such as the Jewish *mikveh*, after the separation is unknown. The roles of Rasta women are certainly changing, due possibly to the practice of polygamy which brings more and more women together. Women have protested the rules of modesty, employment outside the home and involvement in public life. Today many Rasta women, who are supposed to be submissive to their men, no longer cover their heads in public and work in many professional capacities in the Caribbean and globally. What started as a violent anti-White movement has evolved and the Rastafari, walking the streets in their long flowing robes and matted dreadlocks, once feared, by their fellow Jamaicans, are now largely seen as a symbol of righteous living and peace. The movement has come a long way from the days of Leonard Howell in the 1930s, some 88 years later it is a worldwide movement, not always understood, but generally respected.

The connection with Ethiopia and Emperor Haile Selasie has other significances, which create ideological links between that country, Israel and Black Jews. In this instance we are speaking of the *Beta Israel*, some 6,000 Jews who became stranded in Sudan in the 1970's in a time of warfare and famine. The Jews are rescued after the death of the Emperor in 1975 by Prime Minister Menachem Begin (himself a refugee) and the Mosad (BBC News, 2016). These Ethiopian Jews had been forgotten in Ethiopia for over

2,000 years until their exodus and rescue, giving the Rastafari a tangible sign of their claim to the descent from the twelve tribes of Israel.

FROM ZION TO RASTA AND RASTA TO ZION

A more recent phenomenon in the last 20 years is the fascination that the Rastafari faith holds for a number of Jews. With the international celebrity of singers and musical ambassadors such as Bob Marley and his sons Ziggy, Stephen and Junior Gong, roughly two generations of Jews have been exposed to the image, biblical teachings and way of life of Rasta. In the process some Jewish musicians have both adopted portions of the Rasta ideology and have begun to produce the music associated with Rasta worldwide as well as embracing the dreadlocks and the dress of the faith. Among these are the now famous Jewish reggae artist Matisyahu, born Michael Goldwasser, son of a reform rabbi, and the recent *Hatikva6-Hope6* Israeli Reggae band, to name a few. There have been others of course, but Matisyahu in particular stands out because of his international success and fame, and the extent to which he actually looks like one of Marley's sons, Junior Gong, when he is full dreadlocks. For Rastafari, Zion symbolises the real hope of return to the land of milk and honey, Ethiopia. Matisyahu once commented in a video interview that Rasta was singing in their Reggae songs about Zion, yet he was living in Zion, so he could easily identify with their biblical lyrics and aspirations. Matisyahu made the journey to Rasta and back, and has now shaven off his dreadlocks, returning to a more conservative mode of presentation of himself. At the same time as Matisyahu was making his personal and spiritual journey, Ziggy Marley, the son of international Reggae superstar Bob Marley, was moving in the opposite direction from Rasta to Judaism. What Matisyahu brings to Reggae, a musical form lyrically based on the Old Testament of the Bible, is what no Reggae artist can, he has the genetic connection to the land of the Bible. What Ziggy brings to Jewish Reggae is what no Israeli can bring to it genetically, and that is the soul of the Marley brand. Contributing writer, for The Times of Israel, Masimba Musodza, wrote a 2015 article, *The Ties That*

Bind: Reggae, Rastafari, Judaism and Israel. His article around the very topic of this discussion. Young Jews, in touch with celebrity news will already know that Ziggy Marley is married to Israeli, Orli Agai. Their children therefore are Jewish by Halaichic standards. Marley himself has a Jewish heritage through his paternal grandmother. Though distant, this connection has always been significant for Ziggy Marley. He is quoted as saying,

> I've been connected to Israel from when I was a child. Through my father, my mother, we have a strong belief in the history. If you've heard of my father…you've heard of Exodus…We are strongly connected to the history of Israel and feel a very spiritual and personal connection to that land and the people of that land. So this is an honor and a blessing and we will continue to have that connection no matter what anybody says or does and continue to support Israel. (Musodzi, 2015)

Marley was speaking of the honour he felt in receiving the 2015 Jewish National Fund's Shalom Peace Award for his contributions to Israel. Marley's connections to Israel he says is not just his hyphenated heritage, his marriage to a Jewess, but also his background and Rastafari teachings have led him to convert to Judaism. Goldwasser aka Matisyahu and *Hatikva6-Hope6* have had relative success to their claim as well. Goldwasser first heard Bob Marley playing on his dad's stereo and identified with the biblical lyrics, which he saw as clearly Jewish. Since then he has produced six albums - "Dub Side of the Moon," "Radiodread," and "Easy Star's Lonely Hearts Dub Band." And two tributes in reggae to the late Michael Jackson, under the label *Easy Star All-Stars*. He sees Israel as the next big reggae scene. (Retrieved from: Easy Star All-Stars,). *Hatikva6 - Hope6*, the newest of the lot, has found their visit to Marley's home a revelation of how much Rastafari borrows from Judaism.

There is now a body of sites, articles, and contributions that highlight the connections between Rastafari and Judaism, many of which are being promoted by Jews (Schienfield, 2012). A new course to be found on the Darshan Yeshiva site is, *Connections Between Rastafari and Judaism* taught by Benjamin Kweskin (https://darshanyeshiva.org/rastas-and-jews-benjamin-kweskin/). There is likely to be more, not less of this cultural and spiritual interchange. Perhaps this is a small part of the spirituality that other sources point to as the way forward for the youth (Jewish and otherwise) who are drawn to the cultural-spiritual expressions of Judaism but avoid the religious. While Jews and Reggae Rastafari are coming together through music and cultural symbolism, there is another concerted effort being made in the Caribbean and around the world to bring Jews into a Halachic experience of the faith, whether they be Jews by birth or conversion. At the same time, the Chabad is on the move in the Caribbean and they are ministering to cruise-ship loads of Jews.

CHABAD IN THE CARIBBEAN

The Chabad-Lubavitch movement has been the latest addition to the Jewish Caribbean story and has sought to reinvigorate Jewish cultural and religious practice through the introduction of services, destination weddings and *bar mitzvah*, Sunday schools and kosher restaurants. They can presently be found in Puerto Rico, Virgin Islands, Dominican Republic, Martinique, Jamaica, Cayman, Aruba, Dutch Antilles, Grenada, St Barthes, Curacao, Barbados, and Bahamas. The wide reach of their mission speaks to the ever-growing revival of Jewish practice in these islands. (Chabad.org). I had the opportunity of speaking with Rabbi Yakov Raskin, in Jamaica, where he is responsible for the Chabad community. Interestingly, the affable and accessible Rabbi Raskin also said at the beginning of our telephone conversation that he had met every Jew in the island. I pointed out to him that we had not met. I think it was a case of youthful enthusiasm getting the best of his accuracy.

Raskin says Chabad's mission is love. He explains that the word Chabad needs to be understood if we are to understand their mission worldwide. Chabad is an acronym for the Hebrew words that mean 1) wisdom, 2) comprehension and 3) knowledge. Lubavitch is the name of the Russian town where the movement was started and means, "brotherly love". Raskin is understandably proud of the work they have carried out in the Caribbean, having set down roots in fourteen territories with seven of those being established in the last four years. Much of the work they carry out is destination bar/bat mitzvahs and weddings. Located as they are in one of the major cruise ship, tourist destination of Montego Bay, in Jamaica, the movement is ideally placed for receiving large numbers of visitors. Raskin is happy to announce that the last *pesach* – Passover, surpassed the previous ones with an attendance of close to 800 persons, due primarily to the near destruction of the island of Puerto Rico by hurricane Maria in September, 2017. The movement consists of 5,000 Rabbis in 101 countries worldwide. They are Orthodox and therefore follow the tradition of Jews being those born of a Jewish mother. He says that part of the mission of love is to help those Jews who wish to convert to go through the authentic process of coming before the *Beit Din/ Rabbinic Court* of three rabbis and to have the Jewish ancestry properly researched and then the three years of teaching and conversion as per Hasidic Law. Raskin also points to the absence of a *Beit Din* – Jewish Court of Law, or Rabbi in Kingston, the capital city where an active synagogue has existed for over 363 years. Chabad also provides kosher meals to hotels in the Montego Bay area and has a small kosher restaurant, that is becoming increasingly popular. The future of Chabad in the Caribbean is one of putting down firm roots and building a centre that can both service the local community and visitors to this and other islands in the Caribbean where they have offices. The young Rebbi speaks of the prophecy in Isaiah.

> And I will set a sign among them, and I will send those that escape of them unto the nations, to Tarshish, Pul, and Lud, that draw the bow, to Tubal, and Javan, to the isles afar off, that have not heard my fame, neither have seen my glory; and they shall declare my glory among the Gentiles. (Yeshayahu – Isaiah, 66:19 King James Version)

This is not the first attempt on the part of Chabad to create a permanent home in the islands. In Jamaica they have been in and out for a number of years. Rabbi Yakov Raskin and his wife are in the Caribbean to stay, to set up home, and to spread what he terms, their mission of *love*.

Rastafari and Chabad represent two very different views on Judaism. However, there is a common psycho-social thread that each of them will have to overcome, and that is the psycho-cultural beliefs each has about purity and ethnicity. As far as I can see the Rastafari's ideology of Black-centric beliefs and some of the early teachings of Edwards (mentioned above) as the founder of the Bobo Ashanti mansion of Rastafari, denounce all things White. The Jew, for many Blacks is another White man. And the universal love preached and practised by many other mansions of Rastafari, and heralded by Ziggy Marley in his now famous song, "Love is My Religion", is absent from other mansions. The either/or approach taken by the White man in his exclusion of the Black man from his human rights, have been reversed and embraced by some within the faith. If in the past "nothing black no good" was the White man's cry, today some Rastafari now hold that, "nothing white no good". Naturally, this is not unique to this religious group, but it is a barrier to better understanding of the Jew, who some claim is a white usurper.

As it relates to Chabad, it would seem to me that the same Orthodox restrictions they have brought to the Caribbean could backfire in islands with fierce national, cultural identities such as Jamaica. I am not surprised that it has taken them so long to set up roots there. Jamaicans, like the Israelis, see themselves as seriously Jamaican, no matter what other hyphenation they add to that branding. The teachings of Chabad if embraced by many Caribbean Jews, would see them being re-converted. This is not only unthinkable, it is impractical and for many, offensive. If Caribbean Jews have no intention of selling off their businesses and making Aliyah, what need do they have of a further rabbinical conversion, in order to be accepted by Chabad. They already accept themselves and their Jewish identity and have paid the price. Whichever the Rabbi at the time of their conversion (for those who converted); for children of Jewish fathers; for those who completed their *bar/bat mitzvah* they would have already been received into the faith. If Chabad continues to assert that these conversions and *bar/bat mitzvahs* are not approved, they are setting themselves up for considerable opposition. It is important to understand and respond to the historical reality of the ex-colonies. Having come out of 400 years of slavery and colonial oppression, Caribbean island nationals are deeply resistant to foreign forces dictating what they must now do in order to be acceptable to non-natives. This is a slippery slope and the Chabad movement may find it needs a partner in the Jewish Caribbean not adversaries. At the moment they have concentrated on the coasts of the islands performing destination weddings and *bar mitzvah*s for the cruise industry and *kosher* catering for hotel guests. These are niche markets that would welcome any Jewish experience, and which may well remain their primary purpose in the Caribbean. The knowledge of the Jewish faith and the adherence to Torah is also a welcome feature, however sensitivity and caution must be exercised in dealing with the local Jewish communities.

Jews in the Caribbean for the most part do not dress any differently from other members of the population. They tend to be conservative in their practices and social interactions. Even with the celebrations for the High Holy Days the festivities are enjoyed with a sense of family and simplicity. Nothing ostensibly differentiates them from their neighbours, except when they are at *shul*. There they enjoy the full experience of what it means to be Jewish in dress and custom. The observable differences that the Rastafari in their robes and paraphernalia present, is as noticeable as the severe black and white Orthodox dress of the Chabad. Both groups want to visibly stand apart. A process of psychological integration in the life of the Caribbean, of going about one's business in the quiet and peace of assimilation, would stand to be ruined by such differences. The ambition of realising oneself as distinctly Jewish, in the islands has been customarily one of living a life that is worthy of *tikun olam and to actively heal the world.*

Chapter 5

JEWISH LIVES, JEWISH LOVES

I arrived at the synagogue, in a Caribbean community that is now barely surviving. The older man who greeted me at the door was quick to ask, where I was from, what was our community like? but most importantly for him "...do you have a minyan?" I was at the same time surprised and informed by the question because it pointed to the low numbers of Jews in that community. They rarely had ten adult Jews in attendance, the requirement for the service. When I shared with him the frequency and attendance of services in my own synagogue the wistful look on his face made me feel as if I were telling fairy tales and legends from the past. This is part of the nature of the Caribbean Jewish experience. In some islands where Jews originally settled, there are now, no know Jewish settlements nor synagogues in use. Instead of assimilation and integration, these communities chose further migration to North America.

FORBIDDEN LOVE

Despite Jewish prohibitions against intermarriage, records from Haiti stand as an example of what has happened in other settlements where Sephardim, Dutch and Ashkenazi Jews married free women of colour and established families. In other instances where the fear of scandal, reprisals or personal embarrassment could be avoided, many simply supported the families they produced out of wedlock and continued to live "upstanding" Jewish lives within their communities. Some early evidence of such illicit relationships between Jews and slaves or freed creole women, is documented in the wills they left behind. Stanley Mirvis, writing in AJS Perspectives, (AJS Perspectives, The Labour Issue, Fall 2013) traces the connections between 300 wills left behind by Jews in Jamaica and Barbados in the 1700s and discovered that 172 of these left money and possessions to their slaves and that 41 of these testators freed their slaves upon their death, the process is referred to as *manumission*." The most likely cause of manumission of enslaved children was biological paternity" (Mirvis, 2013). Often slaves were left as part of the will to other family members, a few were sold. The terms and conditions of the wills also speak to the affection between the Jewish men and their female slaves. Some claim the Jewish offspring and others maintain two homes with the wife and children and the slave or, freed slave and children. The historical reality of such unions, the children produced and inheritances left behind by the 17th century Caribbean Jew, is another piece of the puzzle. I am not suggesting here that all love stores of interethnic unions end well, but a great number of them appear to have enjoyed relative good fortune.

The creolisation of the Caribbean was helped along by the practise of keeping concubines among the imported and enslaved African women and the white and Jewish men. The West Indian society of the 1700s accepted the offspring as a necessary result of life in the colonies. Some argue that the creole offspring provided a source of free labour and were often without any means of protesting. What is agreed is that polygyny was commonplace with traditional families existing alongside concubines and children born out of wedlock (Kempadoo, 2004). In Curacao, it was noted that marriage to relatives among the Dutch Jews was a way of preserving Jewish identity, and a way of preserving the informal caste system of the wealthiest marrying the wealthiest and so forth. The custom of marrying a woman off on her mother's deathbed was continued and was not carried out for companionship or romance. The Jewish men kept their outside liaisons going, which it is noted, provided them with a labour force that required no pay or inheritance and since the mothers were coloureds or blacks, there was no need to include the children in the synagogue. The reason for marriage remaining within the Jewish community was attributed to the fact that Curacao did not have a plantation society, but rather built its economy on trade. The roles of men and women in the Sephardic community of Curacao suffered a reversal from the male dominated society in which concubinage of black and coloured women was a norm to women having the financial and social freedom to choose who they would marry as their offspring would grow up as Jewish in any event. This after 250 years of continuous marriage within the community where "first cousin marriages were typical of the group as a whole" (Van Der Mark, in Momsen ed, 1993, p. 39).

At times the children resulting from these unions became incorporated into the families. One of the most celebrated records of devotion and affection between a slave and a Jew is that of Solomon Franco and Anne. Famously known for the fact that he was one of the few men who lived in the islands as a single man, having his slave Anne, who cared for him with singular devotion and who, despite having been freed, places herself back in his service for another 3 years. The instructions in his will is that Anne should be allowed to leave the estate with the money and belongings he has given to her, without being searched.

The behest in Franco's own words are for her "faithful service". Franco died in 1721 at the age of 31years. Mirvis assumes from this set of unusual requests that Anne has indeed been Franco's concubine. In other instances, such as the 1765 case of Moses Levy Alvarez, a married Jamaican shopkeeper, with a wife and two children leaves his slave woman and their creole daughter, his brand on their shoulder. Another wife, Mrs. Abraham Nunes Henriques was not as lucky as Mrs Moses Alvarez. Their slave woman, Jenny poisoned Mrs. Henriques. While a more fortunate fate befell the concubine of Moses Gomes Fonseca, who in 1795 speaks of the love he has for the children produced with her and leaves them their freedom and an inheritance.

History is a good place to start in examining how much a situation has changed, or how little. Clearly the laws, rules and social norms for romantic relationships have been completely overturned in the 300 plus years since Franco and Anne and their contemporaries of the 1700s. At the same time that is not to say that a virtual utopia has been created in the Caribbean. The 1900s in Curacao saw a change in the industry and oil became a chief source of income. The impact extended to family structures and the fortunes of women changed with the social prohibitions against marrying within the family became more vocal. Today there are still groups in the Caribbean who continue to marry within their own cultural groups. Notable in this matter are the East Indians, the Chinese and some Arabs who have traditionally sought arranged marriages, bringing in brides from overseas. In rare cases among Caribbean Jews there have been such couplings in modern times, but they are exceedingly rare. More usual is the modern, romantic marriage, where people marry for love. And of course, where cupid's arrow will land, nobody knows. However, the love match or the romantic marriage is a fairly recent concept in history. The marriages and concubinage of the 1700s was governed by a completely different set of beliefs about man-woman relationships from the ones we have become familiar with today.

It may be important to note however that between the early practise of marriage and the now modern concept of the romantic partnership, there is the marriage contract. For centuries the idea of marriage was based on the legal contract. "For most of History it was inconceivable that people would choose their mates on the basis of anything as fragile and irrational as love…" (Coontz, 2005, p. 15). People married as a way of ensuring that the three Ps – progeny, property and paternity were protected. The reproductive imperative – progeny – needed to be organised within a social unit, to make the claiming of children, for the continuation of the family name. The property of family needed to be passed down in an organised fashion and alliances to preserve wealth were important for good social order. Additionally, women and their offspring – like other property, who had no civic rights, needed to be cared for along with their inherited wealth. Marriage was conceived of as a means of ensuring the welfare of women, and as a means of them enjoying the benefits of patriarchy. Finally, paternity was made more secure by the institution of marriage because in law, even if the biological paternity of the offspring of the woman was in doubt, the children born within a legal marriage were deemed to be the product of that marriage, unless otherwise proven. So essentially the original intent of the marriage contract was for the provision and protection of women, while they provided domestic and reproductive benefits to the man so that his name could be passed down. The notion of a love-bond was not at all in question at the start of the marriage enterprise.

To what do we owe this idea of marriage as a result of romantic love? To the era of the troubadours in France and later throughout Europe where they would go from town to town, inventing and playing romantic ballads and stories to entertain the towns people. This is not to say that love did not exist before now, love has always existed, but love was not a sufficient reason for the serious business of marriage contracts, the exchange of property and the reproduction of children who will carry a family's name into the future. Love was for liaisons, concubines, mistresses, secret loves, any relationship outside of the serious business of marriage. Approximately 200 years ago, and 100 years since those early concubine stories of Caribbean Jewry, the Western World began to view the marriage unit as a self-sustaining system in which most of our needs would be met. The industrial revolution made us less dependent on each other and gave us a greater need to have "the one" who would come along and complete us. "In this Western Model, people expect marriage to satisfy more of their psychological and social needs than ever before" (Coontz, 2005, 23). With a higher premium on what marriage has to deliver we are more inclined to fight for the love we want, instead of settling for the Jewish partner that is available.

THE PRESENT SITUATION

It may be surprising for some to know that even within the Rabbinical tradition there is no consensus on the matter of interethnic marriage. And while marriage itself is on the decline all over the world, in the U.S. A. interethnic couples are choosing to marry less often than live together. There is a greater degree of differences in the theological positions of Jewish religious leaders. The reform movement for example, originating out of the Jewish period of Enlightenment in Germany, takes a very liberal view to gender, sexual diversity and inter-ethnic marriages. They are considered to be at the extreme of Jewish liberal thought and do not represent the views of Orthodoxy, so when an Orthodox Rabbi speaks up in favour of Jewish intermarriage, maybe we should pay attention a little at least. Rabbi Avram Mlotek of Base Hillel, offers this opinion in his article, "Time to Rethink our Resistance to Intermarriage" in the New York Jewish Week (http://jewishweek.timesofisrael.com/time-to-rethink-our-resistance-to-intermarriage/) of Wednesday, June 6th, 2018. "If our traditional communities do not learn how to adapt to modernity and cater religiously to different people's needs, Judaism risks nearing its extinction date". This is the same proposition that I have been putting forward in this work. Because I believe it to be true, because I think Caribbean and other histories of diaspora have shown us the value of intermarriage and because it is already what has kept Judaism alive globally. Rabbi Mlotek's community may be largely millennials, but they cannot be dismissed. As he rightly points out, we forget that the period in which anti-semitism was rewarded, was only a mere 70 years ago. He continues by saying, "Gone are the days when dogma and devotion rule; today every Jew is a Jew by choice." This may seem a very radical view for him to take, given he is a Rabbi, but he is clearly also a pragmatist. The world has already changed, and we have to catch up. He remembers his own great-grandfather who mourned one of his daughters upon learning that she had married a non-Jew and sat *shiva – period of mourning,* for her. There are numerous such stories and the pendulum swings both ways. Not only do Jewish families reject non-Jews but the reverse is also true. In an account titled, "I married a Jew" one American woman told her story of shame and isolation on both sides of the family because of her decision to marry a Jewish man. Despite the consequences, in the United States the Pew Research Centre has shown the decline in marriages among Jews overall. Further, that those who do marry almost half marry non-Jews (Pew Research Centre, 2013). These trends for intermarriage are not only present among Caribbean communities.

> 44 percent of married Jews in the United States have a non-Jewish spouse. This number is higher in the Reform and Reconstructionist movements and somewhat lower in the Conservative movement. Intermarriage rarely if ever occurs in the Orthodox community, and when it does happen, people leave for other denominations. (Pew Research Centre, 2013)

Support for intermarriage and conversion is perhaps more widespread than intermarriage itself. Various opinions on the topic were recently aired at a forum for Moment Symposium. Among the views that disagreed with intermarriage was added the usual caveat for conversion to accompany intermarriage. Danny Nevins, Dean of the Rabbinical School and the Division of Religious Leadership at The Jewish Theological Seminary sees the issue as nuanced, and this is the view of many who voiced their opinions in the Symposium. Intermarriage is not ideal, but if you must, then convert.

It's not a binary. Intermarriage has been part of the American Jewish experience since colonial times. It has brought forth blessings and challenges. It is less certain that the children of interfaith couples will identify as Jewish. On the positive side, many wonderful, active and knowledgeable Jews come from an interfaith background and have chosen to exclusively identify with and practice Judaism. In fact, at JTS we have students training to be rabbis and cantors who come from interfaith families which have nurtured their spiritual and Jewish development. We celebrate this fact, without ignoring its rarity. (Nevins in Cooper, 2017).

Most of us can recount some similar tale from the past or from our fore fathers. My own great-grandfather was said to have turned up at the door of the church, shotgun in hand when he learned that his daughter had eloped and was in the process of marrying a negro who worked in the stables on his estate. He was Indian from Bombay and could not tolerate the thought of his daughter and a Black man. He stood outside the barred doors of the church shouting, "I killie the dog", in his broken English. The dog in question being his own daughter, who he would have rather seen dead than married to the wrong kind of man.

Prejudices and the desire for ethnic purity of some sort may never disappear but neither will the practise of inter-ethnic, hyphenated marriages. Two of the men I interviewed shared a small part of their love stories, which are included here. I feel it is important to honour the lives of real flesh and blood people who are the protagonists of these unions. It is easy to imagine that these are simply fairy tales, but they are not, they involve the lives of whole families who are deeply affected by the choices they have to make. Each of them Jewish men who married gentile women. One of these women converted to Judaism and the other attends *shul* but has not converted. All the children from these two marriages have been brought up in the Jewish faith and some have themselves gone on to marry Jews and to raise their own children similarly. They are two brief examples of what regularly happens in Caribbean Jewish families.

ABRAHM BEN EMANUEL & SHOSHANA

We met Abrahm Ben Emanuel earlier in Chapter 3 when we shared his story of being a Jew, what made him existentially Jewish and what he imagines the future of the community in his island-home will be. Now, Abrahm Ben Emanuel tells the story of his late wife, Shoshana who had brought him and his children such great joy, in the very short time that she was with them. Abrahm Ben Emanuel has a lively sense of humour and quick wit. The interview is punctuated by laughter and moments of deep reflection.

> I am evidence of one of the great love stories. Including marrying a woman that was different from what would have been expected for me, and for her also. My mother was very liberal in her thinking, not that she expected me to get married at 18 or 17. Apart from anything else, there were no Jewish girls in the island. I had a Jewish girlfriend in England, but she made the unfortunate mistake of going after a young man from another island (He chuckles). This was her great loss (Laughs).

He is laughing at his youth and the fact that the girl in question had chosen another Caribbean native. He laughingly declares it her loss, because of course she gave him up for someone less impressive. Abrahm Ben Emanuel is now in his 79th year, he is physically agile, his mind is quick and his eyes twinkle with mischief. He reminisces about his late wife, a Catholic, and their early years of their relationship, and the decision they made to marry.

> Shoshana and I never had a relationship outside of marriage. Many people [Jews] had relationships, common law relationships and never married, the moirés of the time never allowed them to marry. Others married and brought up their legitimate children and had outside children and brought up their illegitimate children. People had children within the marriage and had a mistress, and sometimes there were cases of two homes. There was assimilation, basic assimilation. If you lived in the country areas and there was no one else who was Jewish, you hung out with someone

else. I was able to transcend unspoken boundaries, and there *were* unspoken boundaries.

Abrahm Ben Emanuel and Shoshana moved to the capital city in their island and their lives changed immediately from the sleepy rural life to the hustle and bustle of the town. He was 24 years old and she was 27 when they got married.

> When Shoshana and I came to the capital I became Vice President for 10 countries for B'nai B'rith (Children of the Covenant) and I travelled, and I met people who were amazing, and who lived their Judaism without sticking it in your face. And it was a philosophy, that's part of the difference I have. And I had a wonderful woman who also worked with me, went with me, travelled with me. And so, I had a wonderful life. She sat on the head table at the banquet for 600 people in Mexico City, 6 weeks before she died. She had brain cancer, she couldn't see very well, she was amazing. She said she would go with me and she came. 600 people and she sat beside the President of Mexico's sister. I couldn't have asked for more. And I was involved in the days when Zionism is racism in '76. In '78 she died, and I gave up B'nai B'rith when she died, I couldn't manage both.

Abrahm Ben Emanuel has reconciled himself to the loss over the many years since his first wife's passing, at the same time he honours her memory by the respect, affection and admiration he still holds for her. He remarried many years ago and his children are now grown women with families of their own.

SETH AND LINDA

Seth is conservative in his approach to dating and admits that as he got older, there were few single Jewish girls around. He and his wife Linda grew up in the same social circles and eventually dated. They have two children, a daughter and a son, who have also been brought up in the faith.

My wife is Catholic, a lot of Caribbean Catholics are Jews. I think it is more basic than that [why I married outside the faith] I grew up in the 70s and there were a lot of Jewish girls for me to choose from and some of my girlfriends were Jewish. In the later 70s a lot of them migrated and there were maybe two Jewish girls, there were not a lot of Jewish girls to marry and even fewer that you like. Therefore, you looked for a girl you like and because you grew up in a multi-cultural society, sometimes good social relations were a priority. So, you looked for someone that you got along with and were comfortable with socially. Then those of us who hold our Jewishness as important, we would then ask that the children be brought up in the faith. So, if that is what will happen in the future, then there is a possibility for the community's survival. In terms of their way of survival, I think it is more important for you to marry someone whose thinking and cultural and social norms are ones that you can go along with rather than bringing someone from abroad that can't fit in with your culture and it end in disaster. My wife attends *shul* but she has not expressed a desire to convert. We have a son and a daughter who attend.

Seth emphasises the compatibility component in choosing a marriage partner, over whether the person is Jewish or not. He may also see cultural compatibility as important having seen how Jewish women from other cultures have had a very hard time fitting into the Caribbean Jewish culture. He confirms what Arbell (2000) and others have documented the practice among Caribbean Jews to intermarry and to continue to bring up the children in the faith.

Chapter 6

CONCLUSION

Simon Shama begins his documentary series, *The History of the Jewish People*, by showing a montage of photographs of Jews of every complexion and mixture. With each photo he intones, "This is a Jew", until the camera fixes its gaze on his face, "And I am a Jew". It is not the first time that I have seen a documentary that begins with the faces of Jews of all declensions'. Actually, it seems to be in the Jewish consciousness of some, that Jews differ in their appearance even when they have a unifying belief. I thoroughly enjoyed Shama's documentary and look forward to his chronicling not only the exodus to the Americas, but also to Latin America and the Caribbean, where I daresay he will have to show yet another montage of faces, all of whom reflect the diversity of this tiny necklace of islands.

100% JEWISH 100% CARIBBEAN

It seems we have complicated the relationship between Jewish identity, practise and ethnicity to the point where we now have close to half of all those who identify as Jews, refraining from any associations with the faith. The disenchantment with religious practise is not unique to Judaism but there is the additional obstacle that we have to clear, the halachic laws of

Jewish maternal descent. The divisions create further distance between those who have come to Judaism through a variety of other means. For descendants of Jewish fathers and converts, to be considered only semi-acceptable, is to not be accepted at all. While the future of religions is perhaps not very bright, the future of spirituality on the other hand, is brighter. This may well mean that the Jew of the future will be a cosmopolitan spiritualist with Jewish cultural practices. It remains to be seen. In Israel for example, where there is a multi-cultural Jewish state, we could expect that levels of Jewish religious identification would be high, yet there are contradictions in how individuals identify across religious identity, national identity and secular identity. The picture is somewhat complicated. Although a majority of Israelis say they are both religious and Jewish, just under half of them also say they are secular. They think of themselves first as Israelis and then as Jewish, placing their national identity above what they may view as their ethno-religious identity. While Orthodox Jews see themselves first as Jewish and then as Israeli (Pew Research Centre, 2006). Caribbean Jews may also see their island identity as the primary factor in their various aspects of identity. Even in describing each other they refer to Haitian Jew, Jamaican Jew Curacao Jew etc., Identity after all is never one-dimensional.

THE ETERNAL BOND – THE MIND, BODY AND SOUL

Psychology literally means the study of the psyche or soul. Jewish religious belief regarding the five levels of the soul identifies five different levels. The *Nefesh* – soul – drives the physical life of the individual, while the *Ruach* – spirit – is the emotional aspect of the individual, which determines the personality. The *Neshamah* – breath – is the intellect and the *Chayah* – life – is the rational part of ourselves, finally the *Yechidah* – singularity – unites the soul with its source, with G_d. Our understanding of the word soul, has changed from the original Greek word *psyche*, especially in English speaking contexts, to one that excludes the cognitive, the intellect and the personality, and has perhaps been reduced to the concept of breath –

r*uach* and *yechidah* – that which unites with G_d. Psychology itself since the *Principles of Psychology*, by William James, has moved away from the more philosophical beginning to one that is neurological, and behavioural in its efforts to be more scientific. As far back as Aristotle the question of the soul has occupied philosophers and theologians. For him the soul was the self, the identity, the *I am* of the individual and that part that made him Aristotle. He affirmed, "I am my soul". Later Thomas Aquinas, theologian and philosopher rejected Aristotle's claim in asserting for himself that he and his soul were not one. This is an essential position for resurrection theology, because without the soul as a separate entity from the flesh of the body, there would be no *yechidah* to return to G_d. There is an essential logic to this argument. Aquinas is followed years later by Rene Descartes who famously puts forward the idea that the only way to know that we really exist is through our thought, "*cogito ergo sum - I think therefore I am*". And so, the Cartesian theory is born and stays with us today, Descartes's *chayah* (life – is the rational part of ourselves) does not however leave behind the soul. He admits to being both mind and soul, therefore the concept of the psyche is still very much with us up to this point. The final break with the notion of the soul as part of the psychological endeavour came about with William James who removes the soul from his consideration of the science of mental illness and proclaims that he feels free to discard the word soul, preferring to identify the emerging science with the study of behaviour and brain (Grim, https://www.youtube.com/watch?time_continue =3&v=H1lnMEypWBk).

This radical change in the way the human self was understood is what we now recognize as the science. However, in equal measure with the trend towards behaviourism, there has been a counter balance in other circles, away from the purely objective, empiricist approach. Phenomenological psychology (Husserl, 1925) seeks to address this imbalance through the recognition of the importance of the objective experience as part of the life-world of an individual and indeed the life-world of individuals as a universal, who share common perceptions, thoughts and interpretations of the world around them. Rather than a threat to objective psychology, phenomenological psychology opens up the inner world of the individual, if you like, in a rather Cartesian manner, by honouring the inner self, the subjective experiences of the mind as it makes meaning of the world around it. The connection between phenomenological psychology and the soul and Judaism is quite simply to be found in the lived experiences of the Caribbean Jews and others. My life as a Jew, my embodiment of *tikun olam - heal the world*, my acceptance of Mosaic law as the foundation for this lived experience, whether philosophically, spiritually, religiously, or literally, is my Jewish identity. I believe this is the essential message that Abrahm Ben Emanuel, Seth, Miriam and Rueben share when they speak to the question, "What makes you a Jew?". And to the extent that we can recognize the universality of those individual, intersubjective realities, as common to a vast many Jews globally, we can also recognize them as valid acts of identity.

THE FUTURE OF JUDAISM IN THE CARIBBEAN

The late Franklin Krohn, who taught business administration at the State University of New York College at Fedonia, in his travel article in the Jewish American Archives, dismisses the very existence of Jews in the Caribbean from the very title, *In Search of the Elusive Caribbean Jews*. He like other *ethnicists* hold a very pessimistic view of the future of Judaism in the Caribbean. He points to the remote location of the Caribbean away from Jewish influences of Europe but ignores the Jewish settlement of New Amsterdam/New York. The U.S. lies within relatively easy reach of the islands, and Florida, which is replete with Caribbean nationals. His article is a history of exodus from the Caribbean, a people in fear of developing, "a strong Jewish consciousness"; islands with active synagogues but no real Jews to sustain a future. Krohn presents a rather apocalyptic view of the future of the Caribbean Jew.

> Barring some catastrophe that would force Jews once again to seek a haven in the region, it appears that the elusive Jews of the Caribbean will

be little more than a footnote to history, presenting unanswerable questions in the search about their sojourns there. (Krohn, 1993)

While acknowledging that the communities in the Caribbean were secure enough to establish synagogues, that are in use to the present day by persons who self-identify as Jews and have Jewish lineage, Mr. Krohn, has difficulty identifying many Jews at the time of his writing. It seems his assertions are largely based on the Orthodox view that only an individual born of a Jewish mother can be considered a Jew, and further that this Jewish mother is not Jewish by conversion but rather by ethnicity. To be fair, he is not alone in this view. However, rules of race and ethnicity have never held constant, groups have and will continue to apply their favoured measures to what constitutes the group they wish to protect from ethnic pollution. Whites throughout history have gone to remarkable extents to preserve ethnic purity, the Nazi's have done the same. From the one drop rule in the USA, which determines that any White person who has a single drop of Black blood is Black, and the many attempts to create a pseudospecie of the Jew. Interestingly, in a modern scientific era of DNA testing, some of which is being done among Caribbean Jews (Henriques, 2018), how do we determine the percentage of geographic/ethnic deoxyribonucleic acid that qualifies an individual as Jewish. This is no doubt a question for the near future.

> Man as a species has survived by being divided into what I have called *pseudospecies*. First each horde or tribe, class and nation, but then also every religious association has become *the* human species, considering all others a freakish and gratuitous invention of some irrelevant deity. (Erikson, 1994, p40)

A less pessimistic and measured view is presented by Rabbi Joshua Stanton (2016), a Millennial Interfaith Leader. Stanton suggests that there are at least three options for the future of Jews in general, all of which have significance for the diaspora. He thinks that the way forward may be, "…fracture, unity, or plurality. The path we choose will determine our future for generations to come" (Stanton, 2015). The movement away from traditionally held beliefs among the Reform communities and the evolution they see as a necessary engagement for modern Jews could place them in a category that is seen as non-Jewish, along with any other spirituality-based Judaism. Alternatively, Jews of different strands could conceivable come together accepting their different status and recognition under the traditional precepts. This would place orthodox practices at the centre of Jewish identity. Finally, there is the option, which in my mind seems the most likely, and that is a plural approach to Judaism. The final of the three might actually place orthodoxy at a more distant, yet rarefied position in relation to the other strands of Jewish expression. The Orthodox customs and dress would become even more of a novelty as the community closes ranks. But the world has changed and though the urban consciousness does not reflect rural realities around the world, the changes are greater technology and further urbanisation. And the way we communicate and share in that Jewish identity will change along with the global consciousness.

The world has begun to look inward again, developing a social conscience with regard to how we use, misuse and distribute the planets wealth. New opportunities for using the resources, and human capital arise every day and people are thinking differently. We have entered the knowledge Age. The age of internet services and congregations internationally, that you can share Shabbat with on your phone is here. And yet some of these very communities argue for separateness and insularity. It simply will no longer be possible and will not likely be the future of the Millennial Jew. Some would say that the social consciousness that points the finger at global warming, waste and degradation of the earth's resources is a new form of humanism, a spirituality that has no particular guidelines or direction. On the contrary, I would argue that it is the necessary intentionality of purpose beyond tradition and religious dogma and towards affirming that we are also *neshamah* – breath and intellect. If we are thinking beings then we must of necessity, move toward preservation, rather than destruction. In the personal, the spiritual and the public spheres. When we express and experience ourselves as 100% Jewish and 100% Caribbean we are also forced to respect and acknowledge the ways in which others are free to experience themselves. We really cannot spend our lives waiting for someone else to give us the permission to express our full identity, and in the same breath, we cannot take it away from others. It really is about choice and the integrity to live up to that choice. It really is not possible to deny someone their identity as Viktor Frankl knew, with certainty in the concentration camps, even in the worst of times, it is our existential freedom and indeed responsibility to choose. "Everything can be taken from a man but one thing: the last of the human freedoms—to choose one's attitude in any given set of circumstances, to choose one's own way" (Frankl, 2006, p. 66). This is not a choice I can give away to someone else to exercise on my behalf. The answer, to the question of identity is not "Who do you say I am?" but rather a choice, an assertion of "Who I say I am".

REFERENCES

Abraham-Van Der Mark, E. (1993). Marriage and concubinage among the Sephardic merchant elite of Curacao. In Momsen. J. H. (Ed.). *Women and Change in the Caribbean*. Indiana: Indiana University Press.

Adler, R., Proctor II, R. (2010). *Looking out looking in*. 13th ed. California: Wadsworth Publishing.

Alleyne, M. (2002). The Construction and Representation of Race and Ethnicity in the *Caribbean and the World*. University of the West Indies Press: Barbados, Jamaica, Trinidad and Tobago.

Allport, G. (1961). *Pattern and growth in personality*. New York: Holt, Reinhart and Winston.

Antler, J. Gender stereotypes on television. *My Jewish Learning*. https://www.myjewishlearning.com/article/gender-stereotypes-in-television/

Arbell, M. (2000). *The Portuguese Jews of Jamaica*. Kingston: Canoe Press.

Arbell, M. (2002). *The Jewish nation of the Caribbean: the Spanish-Portuguese Jewish settlements in the Caribbean and the Guianas*. Jerusalem: Gefen Publishing House.

BBC. (2009). *Religions at a glance*. Retrieved from: http://www.bbc.co.uk/religion/religions/rastafari/ataglance/glance.shtml.

References

BBC News. (2016). *Saving The Forgotten Jews*. Retrieved from: https://www.youtube.com/watch?v=7MkhKd2rP-A&t=25s

Bennett, R. G. The History of the Jews in the Caribbean. Sefarad.org. Retrieved from: http://sefarad.org/lm/011/jewcar.html

Binford, L. R. (1968). *New perspectives in archeology*. (Eds.). Sally R. & Lewis R.

Boteach, S. (2018). Roaming with the Rastas. *The Jerusalem Post*. Retrieved from: http://www.jpost.com/Opinion/Op-Ed-Contributors/Roaming-with-the-Rastas.

Buriel, R. (1987). Ethnic labeling and identity among Mexican American. In J. S. Phinney & M. J. Rotherram eds. *Children's ethnic socialization: pluralism and development*. 134-52. Newbury Park: Sage.

Burke, P. (2008). Cultural history. In Bennett and Frow (Eds). *The sage handbook of cultural analysis*. Los Angeles, London, New Delhi, Singapore: Sage Publications.

Burns, Sir A. (1954). *History of the British West Indies*. London: George Allen & Unwin.

Branden, N. (1980). *The psychology of romantic love*. New York: Penguin Random House.

——— . *Objectivism*. Kindle Edition.

Brathwaite, K., Anthony O. (1968). Jews: *The people who came*. Kingston: Carlong (Caribbean) Publishers.

Canclini, N. (1990). Hybrid Cultures. (English Tr. Minneapolis: University of Minnesota Press, 1995) in Burke. *Cultural History*. In Bennett & Frow. (Eds). *The sage handbook of cultural analysis*. Los Angeles, London, New Delhi, Singapore: Sage Publications.

Carpenter K. Devonish, H. (2008). *Race, language and self-concept in Caribbean Childhoods*. Kingston: CARIMENSA - University of the West Indies.

Carpenter, K. (2017). (Ed.). *Interweaving Tapestries of Sexuality & Culture*. London: Palgrave Macmillan.

Chevannes, B. (1994). *Rastafari: Roots and Ideology* (Utopianism & Communitarianism). Syracuse: Syracuse University Press.

Clarke, S. (2008). Culture and Identity. In The Sage Handbook of Cultural Analysis. (Eds). *The sage handbook of cultural analysis.* Los Angeles, London, New Delhi, Singapore: Sage Publications.

Coontz, S. (2005). *Marriage, A History: How Love Conquered Marriage.* New York: Penguin Books.

Delva. J. G. 2016. *Hurricane Matthew toll in Haiti rises to 1,000 dead, buried in mass graves.* Oct, 9. https://www.reuters.com/article/us-storm-matthew-haiti-idUSKCN12A02W.

Diner, H. R. (1995). *In the almost promised land: American Jews and Blacks 1915 a 1935.* Johns Hopkins UniversityPress. Revised ed.

Dvorin, Dani. (1998). Parallelisms and differences: Rastafarianism and Judaism. *The Dread Library.* Retrieved from: https://debate.uvm.edu/dreadlibrary/dvorin.html.

Erikson, E. H. (1980). *Identity and the Life Cycle.* New York: W. W. Norton & Company.

———. (1994). *Identity Youth and Crisis.* New York: W. W. Norton & Company.

Fanon, F. (2008). *Black Skins White Mask.* Revised ed., Grove Press: New York.

Franco, S. AJS Perspectives. The faithful service: enslaved domestic labor in the homes Of West Indian Sephardim. *The magazine of the association for Jewish studies.* Retrieved from http://perspectives.ajsnet.org/the-labor-issue-fall-2013/the-faithful-service-enslaved-domestic-labor-in-the-homes-of-west-indian-sephardim/

———. (1980). *Identity and the Life Cycle.* New York: W. W. Norton & Company.

Frank, B. G. (2004). *A travel guide to the Jewish Caribbean and South America.* Kingston: Pelican Publishers.

———. (2006). *Jamaica's tiny Jewish community marks 350 years.* The Jerusalem Post. October 26.

Frankl, V. E. (2006). Man's search for meaning. Boston: Beacon Press 1st ed. Gerber, J., Pinto. P. M. (2013). *The Portuguese Jewish legacy. JBS.* Retrieved From https://www.youtube.com/ watch?v=f6WcQGn5Xk4&t=2629s .

Gerszberg, C. O. (2007). In Cuba, finding a tiny corner of Jewish life. *The New York Times*. Jews of Cuba. Retrieved from: https://www.nytimes.com/2007/02/04/travel/04journeys.html.

Gilman, S. L. (1995). Freud, Race and Gender. In *Jewish explorations of sexuality*. (Ed.). Jonathan Magonet. Providence & Oxford: Berghahn Books.

Girvan N. (2005). Reinterpreting the Caribbean. in Pantin (Ed.). *The Caribbean economy, a Reader*. Kingston: Ian Randle Publishers.

Google.com. (2018). *Map of the Caribbean*. Retrieved from: https://mail.google.com/mail/u/0/?tab=wm#inbox.

Goffman, E. (1956). *The presentation of self in everyday life*. University of Edinburgh Social Science Research Centre. Edinburgh. Monograph No.2.

Gruber, R. E. (2002). *Virtually Jewish: Reinventing Jewish culture in Europei* University of California Press.

Hall, S., Schwarz, B. (2017). *Familiar stanger: A life between two islands*. Durham and London: Duke University Press.

Hakai Magazine. *Synagogues*. June 15. Retrieved from: https://www.smithsonianmag.com/travel/Caribbean-synagogue-sand-floor-180963581/#yKPpAeB7j4bwy8Ul.99.

Henriques, F. (1957). *Jamaica: Land of wood and water*. London: McGibbon and Kee.

Herzig, S. (2012). *Jewish culture & customs*. (Kindle locations 1587-1588). The friends of Israel gospel ministry, Inc. Kindle Edition.

Hintzen, P. (2002). Race and creole ethnicity in the Caribbean. In Shepherd & Richards (Eds.). *Questioning creole: Creolisation discourses in Caribbean culture*. Kingston: Ian Randle Publishers.

Husserl, E. (1925). *Phenomenological psychology*: Lectures, summer semester, 1925.

Scanlon, J. Translator). Springer; Softcover reprint of the original 1st ed. 1977 ed.. Jewishwikipedia.info. (2018). *The Caribbean – Jamaica*. Retrieved from: http://www.jewishwikipedia.info/jamaica.html.

Jewishwikipedia. *The incredible story of the Jews. The Caribbean – Jamaica.* (Retrieved from: http://www.jewishwikipedia.info/jamaica.html .

Juro, R. A. *A visit to the Jews of Suriname.* The Jewish Press. Vol. 6. 21. 13 Issue.

Kertzer, M. N., *What is a Jew?* New York: Collier Books, Macmillan Publishing, 4th ed.

Kritzler, E. (2009). *Jewish pirates of the Caribbean.* New York: Doubleday.

Krohn, F. B. (1993). The search for the elusive Caribbean Jews. *American Jewish archives.* Retrieved from: http://americanjewisharchives.org/publications/journal/PDF/1993_45_02_00_krohn.pdf .

Henriques, F. (1957), Land of Wood & Water. McGibbon & Kee: London.

Lasser, J. (1994). *Gender role socialization in Jewish men.* Presented at the 102nd annual APA convention.

Lang, B. (2005). Hyphenated-Jews and the anxiety of identity. *Jewish social studies,* Volume 12, Number 1, Fall 2005 (New Series), pp. 1-15.

Lapin, D. (2014). Update by Rabbi Douglas Lapin. *Jewish and kosher Haiti.* Retrieved from: http://www.kosherdelight.com/Haiti.htm.

Lewis, G. K. (1968). *The growth of the modern West Indies.* New York: Monthly Review Press.

Meyer, M. A. (1972). *The origins of the modern Jew: Jewish identity and European culture in Germany, 1749-1824.* Detroit Michigan: Wayne State University Press.

Miller, D. M. (2017). *Half Jew.* Create Space Publishing Platform. Create Space.

Mlotek, A. (2018). Time to rethink our resistance to intermarriage. *The New York Jewish Week.* Retrieved from: http://jewishweek.timesofisrael.com/time-to-rethink-our-resistance-to-intermarriage/. Wednesday, June 6th, 2018.

Musodzi, M. (2015). The ties that bind: Reggae, Rastafari, Judaism and Israel. *The Times of Israel.* November 30, 2015.

My Jewish Learning. *My Jewish cultural identity.* Retrieved from https://www.myjewishlearning.com/article/jewish-cultural-identity/.

Nevins, D. (2017). Is intermarriage good for the Jews? *A moment symposium*. In Cooper, M. Retrieved from: https://www.moment mag.com/intermarriage/.

Pew Research Centre. (2013). *A portrait of Jewish Americans: Findings from a Pew Research Center Survey of U.S. Jews.*

Pew Research Centre. (2016). *Israel's religiously divided society. Religion and public life*. http://www.pewforum.org/2016/03/08/israels-religiously-divided-society/.

Phillips Casteel, S. (2016). *Calypso Jews: Jewishness in the Caribbean literary imagination*. Columbia: Columbia University Press.

Podzkiewitz, J. (2007). *Jewish heritage on Curacao*. Posted March 2, 2007. Retrieved from: https://www.youtube.com/watch?v=uszBhn 6IljE.

Pollard, Velma. (2000). *Dread talk*. Toronto: McGill-Queen's University Press Repeating Islands. (2018). *Blending Caribbean sun and Jewish history in Curaçao. News and commentary on Caribbean culture, literature, and the arts*. April 20. (https://Repeatingislands.Com/2018/04/20/Blending-Caribbean-Sun-And-Jewish-History-In-Curacao/)

Salzberg, E. (2009). *Connections between Judaism and Rastafarianism*. Retrieved from: https://debate.uvm.edu/dreadlibrary/Salzberg.htm.

Samuel, W. F.1936. A review of the Jewish colonist in Barbados in the year 1680. *The Jewish Historical Society of England*. London: Purnell & Sons.

Sartre, J. P. (1956). *Existentialism from Dostoyevsky to Sartre*. (Ed.). Kaufman, W. Translator: Mairet, P. Meridian Publishing Company. Retrieved from: https://www.marxists.org/reference/archive/sartre/works/exist/sartre.htm.

Schama, S. (2014). *The story of the Jews with Simon Schama*. DVD release May 6, 2014.

Schinefield, M. (2012). *Reggae's Jewish connection. Shmooze: your Jewish pop culture fix*. Retrieved from: https://forward.com/schmooze/161916/reggaes-jewish-connection/).

Schuessler, R. (2017). *Why sand covers the floor of one of the Western Hemisphere's oldest synagogues*. Smithsonian.com. Retrieved from:

https://www.smithsonianmag.com/travel/Caribbean-synagogue-sand-floor-180963581/

Shomron, Y. (2010). *The Last Jew in Haiti*. Retrieved from: https://www.youtube.com/watch?v=UV91JOc34JM&t=4s.

Smith, M. G. (1965). *The plural society in the British West Indies*. CA: University of California Press.

Sombart, W. (2015). *The Jews and modern capitalism*. CT: Martino Fine Books.

Stanley M. (2013). "The Faithful Service": Enslaved Domestic Labor in The Homes of West Indian Sephardim. AJS Perspectives. *The Magazine of the Association for Jewish Studies*.

Stanton, Rabbi Joshua. 2016. *"Are You Jewish?: Judaism and the Future of Faith"*. HuffPost.com. Retrieved from: https://www.huffingtonpost.com/joshua-stanton/are-you-jewish-judaism-and-the-future-of-faith_b_7213570.html).

Taglioni F., Cruse, R. (2012). Is Suriname a Caribbean Island like the others? In Cruse & Rhiney (Eds.). *Caribbean Atlas. Retrieved from* http://www.caribbean-atlas.com/en/themes/what-is-the-caribbean/is-suriname-a-caribbean-island-like-the-others.html.

Taylor, P., Case. F. I. (Eds.). (2013). *The encyclopedia of Caribbean Religions*: Volume 1: A - L; Volume 2: M – Z. University of Illinois Press. 1st ed.

The Hakluyt Society. (201). The hidden faith project: Jews of Dominican Republic. Retrieved from: https://www.youtube.com/watch?v=PE63cJ8TeIM.

Tortello, R. (2004). Out of many cultures: The Jews in Jamaica. *Pieces of the past*. Kingston: Jamaica Gleaner. Retrieved from: http://old.jamaica-gleaner.com/pages/history/story0054.htm . June 7.

The Great Courses. *Mind body philosophy of the east and west - spiritual dualism in the History of thought*. Retrieved from: https://www.thegreatcoursesdaily.com/history-of-the-soul.

The Economist. (2014). *Jewishness: Who is a Jew: Competing answers to an increasingly pressing question*. International Press: Jerusalem,

London, New York. Jan 11th 2014. https://www.economist.com/international/2014/01/11/who-is-a-jew

The Hakluyt Society. (1813). *Journal of Christopher Columbus*. Retrieved from: https://archive.org/details/journalofchristo00colurich

The Jewish Agency for Israel. *The Law of Return, 5710-1950*. Retrieved from: http://www.jewishagency.org/first-steps/program/5131.

The Knowles Collection. (2017). *The Jews of Haiti. The Knowles Collection: Connecting Jewish families*. 2017. Retrieved from: https://knowlescollection.blogspot.com/2017/02/jews-of-haiti.html.

Weiner, R. *Cuba virtual History Tour*. Retrieved from: https://www.jewishvirtuallibrary.org/cuba-virtual-jewish-history-tour.

Werner, S. (2015). *The Jews and Modern Capitalism*. Epstein, M. Translator. CT: Martino Fine Books. Kindle Edition.

Wilson, J. F. (2008). *Earthquakes and volcanoes: Hot springs*. BiblioLife.

Yoffie, E. H. Rabbbi. (2013). *The self-delusion of secular Jews*. Huffington Post. Retrieved from: https://www.huffingtonpost.com/rabbi-eric-h-yoffie/the-self-delusions-of-secular-jews_b_2479888.html

ABOUT THE AUTHOR

Dr. Karen Carpenter is a Psychologist, and the Editor of *Interweaving Tapestries of Sexuality & Culture*, author of *Love & Sex: The Basics*, and co-author of the upcoming *Language, Race & the Global Jamaican*. She is a research consultant and Adjunct Lecturer in The Institutes of Caribbean Studies and Gender Studies. A Florida Board Certified Clinical Sexologist, she is the Director of The Caribbean Sexuality Research Group (CSRG) Sexology Clinic, at the University Hospital of The West Indies. Dr. Carpenter is the host of Love & Sex for radio and television. Her research interests include: psycholinguistics; the phenomenology of identity; and human sexuality.

INDEX

#

12 tribes of Israel, 76

A

Abraham, 1, 63, 89, 107
adulthood, 2, 31, 50, 55, 56, 63
Alhambra Decree, 9
Aliyah, 7, 78, 84
America, 10, 11, 13, 15, 19, 22, 43, 47, 58, 60, 75, 87, 99, 109
ancestors, 8, 51
Argentina, 11
Ashkenazi, ix, 5, 15, 16, 17, 18, 19, 20, 36, 52, 53, 87
Ashkenazi Jews, ix, 15, 16, 52, 53, 87
assimilation, 1, 3, 7, 9, 13, 18, 25, 36, 39, 41, 43, 56, 85, 87, 95

B

Barbados, 11, 19, 25, 53, 82, 88, 107, 112
Bashevis Singer's, 39
Beta Israel, 1, 79

Bible, 50, 62, 64, 65, 70, 77, 78, 80
Black Code, 13
blackness, 42
Branden, 30, 39, 108
Branden, Nathaniel, ix
Brazil, 5, 11, 13, 14, 19
British and Dutch West India Companies, 11

C

Canada, 17, 21, 35, 44
Caribbean, 2, 3, 5, 6, 7, 9, 10, 11, 13, 14, 15, 18, 19, 20, 21, 22, 23, 25, 27, 34, 35, 39, 40, 42, 43, 47, 48, 49, 51, 52, 53, 56, 58, 61, 71, 73, 74, 75, 76, 79, 82, 83, 84, 85, 87, 88, 90, 91, 92, 94, 95, 97, 99, 100, 102, 103, 104, 107, 108, 109, 110, 111, 112, 113
Caribbean Jew(s), x, xi, 5, 20, 23, 25, 27, 48, 49, 51, 56, 61, 84, 87, 88, 90, 91, 94, 97, 100, 102, 103, 111
Chabad, xi, 62, 66, 69, 72, 73, 82, 83, 84, 85
Chabad-Lubavitch, 82
Christianity, 9, 48, 62, 65, 76
Christians, 10, 23, 65

circumcision, 67
Colombia, 11
Colonial Jews, 22
colonisation, 14
Columbus, Christopher, 9, 10, 12, 15, 21, 114
commerce, ix, 11, 14, 22, 24
consciousness, 99, 102, 104
conservative, 6, 52, 55, 61, 62, 63, 70, 80, 85, 93, 96
Conversos, 9, 10, 14, 16, 18, 23, 53
convert, 6, 9, 48, 62, 65, 68, 81, 83, 93, 97
creole, 39, 42, 44, 88, 89, 110
crypto, 5, 11
Cuba, 11, 16, 17, 18, 19, 110, 114
cultural hybridity, 43
cultural identities, 27, 84
cultural norms, 36, 40
cultural theory, ix
culture, ix, x, xi, 3, 5, 6, 8, 30, 32, 35, 36, 37, 39, 40, 43, 44, 48, 50, 54, 61, 63, 70, 71, 76, 97, 108, 109, 110, 111, 112
Curacao, 11, 13, 15, 48, 53, 82, 88, 90, 100, 107, 112
Czechoslovakia, 13, 53

Eretz Israel, 8
Erikson, Erik H., 2, 5, 31, 55, 103, 109
ethics, 50
Ethiopia, 1, 74, 75, 76, 79, 80
ethnicist(s), 33, 43, 102
ethnicity, 3, 6, 7, 32, 35, 36, 39, 41, 42, 50, 57, 61, 84, 99, 103, 107, 110
exile, 1, 3, 33
existential, ix, 4, 54, 105
exodus, ix, x, 1, 4, 13, 15, 17, 80, 81, 99, 102

F

faith, 10, 36, 43, 48, 56, 57, 58, 61, 64, 66, 67, 70, 74, 76, 78, 80, 82, 84, 94, 96, 97, 99, 113
Fanon, Frantz, 4
fear, 3, 43, 88, 102
five levels of the soul, 100
food, 3, 8, 24, 48, 70, 78, 79
France, ix, x, 4, 13, 16, 25, 91
Frankl, Viktor, 25, 105
French, x, 4, 10, 11, 12, 13, 43
Freud, x, 32, 33, 110

D

deoxyribonucleic acid, 103
diaspora, 3, 7, 10, 24, 35, 62, 92, 103
Dominican Republic, 16, 17, 82, 113
Dutch, x, 10, 11, 13, 14, 16, 21, 25, 36, 53, 82, 87, 88

G

genocide, 34
Germany, ix, x, 13, 17, 52, 67, 68, 92, 111
Glozman, 39
God, 67
Goldwasser, Michael, 80

E

education, 13, 21, 55, 56, 57, 58, 59
Egypt, 13
emotion, 41
English, x, 11, 19, 22, 25, 33, 52, 55, 58, 77, 94, 100, 108

H

hair, 27, 32, 41, 44, 67, 73, 76, 79
Haiti, 11, 12, 13, 17, 87, 109, 111, 113, 114
Halachic tradition, 6
Hasidic (law), 61, 83

Index

Hatikva6, 80, 81
history, 1, 3, 5, 6, 7, 8, 9, 14, 18, 22, 23, 36, 44, 49, 51, 53, 56, 62, 64, 81, 90, 102, 103, 108, 112, 113, 114
holocaust, 13, 19, 53
human, 25, 29, 31, 40, 43, 70, 84, 101, 103, 104
hyphenated identity, x

I

identification, x, 6, 14, 32, 61, 100
identity, vii, ix, x, xi, 2, 4, 5, 6, 11, 14, 22, 25, 27, 29, 30, 33, 34, 35, 36, 37, 39, 41, 42, 49, 52, 54, 56, 58, 61, 62, 63, 64, 66, 68, 69, 71, 72, 84, 88, 99, 101, 102, 104, 105, 108, 109, 111
individuals, ix, 2, 8, 29, 35, 36, 42, 100, 101
inquisition, ix, 5, 11, 14, 18, 19
intermarriage, xi, 1, 17, 18, 34, 36, 42, 56, 87, 92, 93, 94, 111, 112
islands, ix, x, xi, 11, 13, 14, 17, 24, 35, 36, 41, 48, 49, 51, 54, 56, 66, 67, 69, 82, 83, 84, 85, 87, 89, 99, 102, 110
Israel, x, 1, 6, 7, 8, 15, 18, 19, 20, 22, 52, 53, 54, 55, 60, 62, 70, 71, 73, 74, 76, 79, 80, 81, 100, 110, 111, 112, 114

J

Jamaica, 11, 16, 19, 20, 21, 25, 42, 44, 47, 53, 57, 73, 74, 78, 82, 83, 84, 88, 107, 109, 110, 111, 113
Jew by birth, 6
Jew by culture, 6
Jew by religion, 6
Jewish and Black literature, 4
Jewish culture,, 8
Jewish ethnicity, 7
Jewish men, xi, 38, 48, 52, 88, 94, 111
Jewish presence in the Caribbean, 3
Jewish sexual identity, 39
Jewish State, 7
Jewish-ness, 32
Judaism as lineage, ix

L

law, x, 7, 51, 78, 83, 91, 95, 102, 114
Law of Return, 7, 114
laws, 58, 64, 68, 78, 79, 90, 99
love, xi, 10, 11, 36, 39, 50, 63, 82, 83, 84, 88, 89, 90, 91, 94, 95, 108

M

majority, 17, 35, 37, 43, 48, 53, 56, 100
Marley, Ziggy, 80, 84
Marrano, 5, 13
Marranos, 18
marriage, ix, 36, 57, 81, 88, 90, 91, 92, 95, 97
Matisyahu, 80, 81
Mexico, 11, 47, 96
Middle East, 13, 47
migrant population, 35
Millenial, 103, 104
Millenial Jew, 104
mixed race, 41
motivation, 13, 28, 41, 43
multi-ethnic, 32, 34, 35, 58

N

national identity, 5, 100
next generation, 71
North America, 43, 58, 87

O

Operation Cigar, 18

opportunities, 16, 18, 104
orthodox, 6, 7, 51, 53, 62, 63, 64, 76, 79, 84, 85, 92, 93, 100, 103, 104

P

pain, 50
Panama, 13
parents, 56, 62, 79
personal philosophy, 28, 29
personal psychology, 28, 29
personality, 34, 100, 107
phenomenological, 3, 101, 110
phenotype, 3, 32, 36, 41, 44
philosophy, xi, 4, 27, 29, 30, 59, 70, 74, 96, 113
Poland, 13, 53, 66
Polish Jews, 13
population, 4, 6, 11, 13, 14, 18, 20, 35, 53, 85
Portugallo Colon, 21
postcolonial discourse, 42
presenting self, 30, 33, 40
progressive, 6, 17, 52, 57, 58, 61
prosperity, 18, 23, 25, 59
pseudospeciation, 5
psychology, x, xi, 3, 6, 27, 28, 29, 41, 100, 101, 108, 110
psychology of ethnicity, 3
psychoses, 34
psycho-social, x, 2, 22, 84
purity, 43, 79, 84, 94, 103

R

race, 3, 32, 33, 41, 42, 44, 50, 53, 59, 103, 107, 108, 110
racial ambiguity, 32, 44
racial stereotypes, 40
racism, 17, 96

Rastafari, xi, 73, 74, 76, 77, 78, 79, 80, 81, 84, 85, 108, 111
reality, 1, 8, 28, 29, 34, 50, 59, 84, 88
reconstructionist Jews, 6
reform, 6, 52, 55, 63, 71, 80, 92, 93, 103
religion, ix, xi, 3, 6, 39, 48, 65, 71, 74, 76, 107
religious beliefs, 5, 21, 40, 65
Romania, 13
romantic relationship, 37, 90
Roth, Phillip, 40
rules, 41, 79, 90, 103

S

Santo Domingo, 11, 12, 16, 17, 19, 48
school, 13, 18, 19, 20, 47, 48, 55, 56, 57, 59, 64, 69, 82
secular, 6, 29, 62, 71, 100, 114
secular Judaism, 71
self-concept, x, 2, 26, 34, 42, 108
self-esteem, 2, 26, 39
self-identity, 2, 39
Sephardic, ix, 5, 10, 13, 14, 15, 19, 24, 36, 52, 53, 68, 69, 89, 107
Sephardic Jews, 10, 13, 14, 15, 19, 24
services, 19, 22, 62, 63, 69, 82, 87, 104
Shapiro, 39
slavery, ix, 24, 41, 84
society, 31, 37, 40, 41, 42, 59, 88, 97, 112, 113
Sosua, 16, 17
soul, xi, 80, 100, 102, 113
Spanish, x, 9, 10, 11, 12, 16, 18, 19, 20, 58, 62, 107
species, 34, 44, 103
spirituality, xi, 59, 65, 71, 82, 100, 104
stereotypes, 32, 33, 37, 40, 44, 58, 107
Stuart Hall, ix, 42, 75
sugar, ix, 11, 14, 19, 22, 23
sugar plantation, 19, 25

Suriname, 11, 14, 15, 16, 53, 111, 113
survival, x, 9, 16, 21, 25, 39, 44, 97
symbolism, 74, 82
synagogue, 13, 15, 17, 18, 19, 20, 27, 47, 48, 52, 53, 57, 60, 62, 67, 68, 69, 70, 83, 87, 89, 110, 113

T

The 'others', 32
The colour bar, 41
The Cuban Thaw, 19
The other, 1, 5, 7, 17, 19, 24, 32, 33, 37, 39, 41, 74, 76, 94, 100, 104, 113
the perceived self, 30
the real self, 30
trade, ix, 11, 14, 22, 23, 58, 89
Trujillo, 17

U

unions, 36, 45, 88, 89, 94
United States, 4, 12, 13, 15, 18, 21, 35, 36, 56, 75, 93

V

vessels, 23
vision, 29
vocabulary, 42, 70
voice mail, 68

W

war, 15, 17, 18, 19, 33, 53, 60
wealth, 19, 24, 59, 91, 104
West Indies, 3, 13, 22, 24, 107, 108, 111, 113
who is a Jew, vii, x, 1, 6
Who is a Jew Law, 7
World War I, ix, 14, 18
World War II, ix, 14, 18
worldwide, xi, 6, 67, 74, 79, 80, 82

X

xenophobia, 5

The Contemporary Caribbean: Issues, Challenges, and Opportunities

Editor: Clinton Beckford, Ph.D. (Faculty of Education, University of Windsor, Windsor, ON, CA)

Series: Central America and the Caribbean

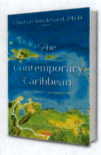

Book Description: *The Contemporary Caribbean: Issues, Challenges and Opportunities* explores a number of contemporary issues facing the Caribbean, which will be of broad interest to a regional and global audience. The book is written from multiple academic perspectives, but with a strong focus on social sciences.

Hardcover ISBN: 978-1-53614-087-3
Retail Price: $230

Following the Northern Star: Caribbean Identities and Education in North American Schools

Authors: Greg Wiggan (University of North Carolina at Charlotte, Charlotte, NC, USA) and Jean T. Walrond (Concordia University College of Alberta and Northern Alberta Institute of Technology, Edmonton, Alberta, Canada)

Series: Education in a Competitive and Globalizing World

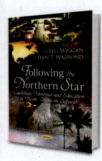

Book Description: This book explores the intersection of migration, identity development and the school achievement of Caribbean heritage children. In doing so, it uncovers the history of the Caribbean and its early inhabitants such as the Siboneyes, Guanahatabeyes, Tainos, Caribs, and Arawaks, who predated the arrival of European explorers and enslavers, and it explains the relevant connections to colonialism, neo-colonialism and Caribbean migration to North America.

Hardcover ISBN: 978-1-62417-597-8
Retail Price: $145